12 Terrible Dog Training Mistakes Owners Make That Ruin Their Dog's Behavior… And How to Avoid Them

by

Suzanne Hetts, Ph.D.
Certified Applied Animal Behaviorist
Co-Owner and President
Animal Behavior Associates, Inc.

Copyright Information

Table of Contents

Disclaimer

Anytime your dog's behavior changes, or doesn't appear to be typical for him or her, your first step is to have your dog evaluated by your veterinarian. The first signs of many medical problems are behavior changes. Don't jump to the conclusion your dog's behavior issue doesn't have a medical cause. A significant percentage of unwanted behaviors – most particularly aggression – are caused by pain and discomfort that have gone unrecognized.

Do not assume the information in this book is specific to your dog's particular behavior or training issue. You should consult a certified applied animal behaviorist to help you analyze and modify your dog's behavior; a veterinary behaviorist is most knowledgeable about particular medications that can be used in conjunction with behavior modification; and certified trainers or non-degreed behavior consultants can also help you implement a behavior modification or training plan.

This book will make you a more educated consumer of behavior and training services, help you evaluate the knowledge level of those people you are considering working with, and allow you to avoid the pitfalls less competent people will not only allow, but drag you into.

Use the information in this book to avoid the terrible twelve training mistakes and to make both you and your dog happier with one another.

I don't like it any better than you, but here's some information to keep the lawyers happy. The author or Animal Behavior Associates, Inc. do not assume responsibility for and make no representation about the suitability or accuracy of the information contained in this work for any purpose, and make no warranties, either express or implied, including the warranties or merchantability and fitness for a particular purpose. Neither shall be held liable for adverse or unwanted reactions to or damage resulting from the application of this information. Animal Behavior Associates, Inc. and the author shall be held harmless from any and all claims that may arise as a result of any reliance on the information provided.

Your Chance to Keep Informed

Because you bought my book, it's obvious you are interested in dog behavior and training. If you want to keep up with the latest advances about how dogs learn, how they think and what they are capable of, I'd like to invite you to subscribe to our e-newsletter "Pet Behavior One Piece at a Time". Each issue contains original articles about not only dog behavior, but people-pet relationships, analysis of current events important to dogs and their owners, summaries of recent research and more.

We don't give cats short shrift – important initiatives are taking place to improve the quality of care cats receive, and how we can better meet their behavioral needs and prevent both medical and behavioral problems.

So visit www.TerribleDogTrainingMistakes.com where you'll find a registration link for our newsletter.

Other free resources we have for you are a series of 10 audio tips on dog and cat behavior. Each week, you'll receive an email with a link to a 3-5 minute audio message containing an important tip about dog and cat behavior. You'll be amazed at how just a few changes in how you interact with your dog and cat can produce huge improvements in their behaviors and in your relationships with them.

Visit www.SensibleDogTraining.com and www.CatBehaviorHelp.com and register to enjoy these unique tips you can listen to while you check your emails.

Don't let your commitment to learning more about your pet's behavior stop with this book. Subscribe to these free resources today.

You'll find links to more resources throughout this book. In addition, the links to all of the references and resources listed in this book can be accessed from www.TerribleDogTrainingMistakes.com.

Acknowledgements

No one writes a book without support and help from a variety of people, and I am no exception. First I'd like to thank Jim Edwards for his writing coaching program which was the primary reason I took on this book writing project. His step by step writing protocol and personal support was why I was able to write the book at all, AND allowed me to finish it in a much shorter time frame and with less brain damage than I ever would have predicted. If you want access to the same protocol and have a book you want to write, I'd encourage you to take advantage of his great program at www.27DayBook.com.

Thanks to the other participants in his coaching program who offered their encouragement when I needed it. We all stuck with it and supported each other through the trials, tribulations, and rough spots on our road to completing our book projects.

Thanks to my husband Dr. Dan Estep for his tolerance when I put other projects on hold, and for taking on more of our "to do" list so I could finish this book.

I sincerely appreciate Fran Berry and Julie Hecht for reading my almost final version and giving me their feedback.

A special thank you to Caroline Wolstenholme for her detailed review and editing suggestions and for looking at the book more than once when saving the file went awry. I'm so lucky to have such a great colleague and Behavior Education Network member!

Love and hugs to my beloved Brandy, Blaze, and Katie, the first dogs I trained for obedience competitions years ago. They unfortunately experienced some of my mistakes early in my career. And to Ashley, our high maintenance Dalmatian who taught us what it's like to live with a difficult dog for 13 years, and reminded us why it's easy for our clients to fall victim to some of the 12 mistakes.

And I can't leave out Mocha, our gentle soul Dalmatian. I used pictures of him as illustrations in several important places in the book.

Thanks to Coral, our current Irish setter, and diva only-dog who makes me laugh and soothes my soul every single day. She epitomizes why and how dogs make our lives better. I think we finally did most everything right with her – no mistakes – and it's paid off big time. Have to give her credit though – she came with good genes!

Finally, thanks to you – the reader – for purchasing the book. I hope it makes your life, your dog's life, and your lives together, better.

About the Author

 My name is Suzanne Hetts and I've been helping people just like you with their pets' behavior and training issues since 1984. I completed my Ph.D. in animal behavior in 1989 and was certified by the Animal Behavior Society as an Applied Animal Behaviorist (CAAB) in 1991.

My major professor and I founded Animal Behavior Associates, Inc. while I was still in graduate school, and my husband and fellow behaviorist Dr. Dan Estep have been ABA's co-owners since 1988. In the years since, we've loved helping thousands of owners understand their dogs better while resolving and managing their dogs' behavior problems.

I was the staff behaviorist – one of the first CAABs to be employed full time at an animal shelter – at the Denver Dumb Friends League for almost four years. I established the first pet behavior helpline at a shelter, and trained volunteers to help new pet owners when they encountered behavior issues in the pets they adopted from the shelter. This help-line received national recognition and the materials I developed formed the basis for the Humane Society of the United States' Pets for Life Program.

I've not only created thousands of customized, individual behavior modification plans for dogs just like yours, but I've also developed training programs for big corporations in the pet industry.

I've had the privilege to speak at animal behavior related conferences on 5 continents, including Australia, North and South America, Europe and Asia, as well as the island of St. Kitts.

I'm the author of one of American Animal Hospital Association's best-selling books, **Pet Behavior Protocols**. I've had my articles appear in popular pet magazines including **Dog Fancy**, **Cat Fancy**, and **Animal Wellness**. For many years, Dan and I wrote a pet column for the **Rocky Mountain News**, answering questions from readers and having the opportunity to educate even more people about the science of animal behavior as it applies to pets.

In my career of almost 30 years helping people and their dogs and cats, I've worked in diverse settings: my private behavior consulting practice Animal Behavior Associates, Inc.; at a large, private metropolitan animal shelter with an international reputation; at the Veterinary Teaching Hospital at Colorado State University; and as an independent consultant for a major pet store chain, two pet food companies, and several pet product companies. That breadth of experience means I understand the needs of dog owners when it comes to helping their dogs be enjoyable and safe members of the family, and how important it is to loving pet parents to provide a quality lifestyle for their dogs.

I also know the need of pet professionals, including veterinarians, dog trainers, behavior consultants, and business owners from grooming salons to day cares, to be able to offer their clients trusted information and education resources.

While I still enjoy working individually with dog and cat owners, Dan and I now spend most of our time reaching more pet owners and pet professionals online through our websites listed below.

On a personal level, my family has always included a dog since I was five years old. My love for cats came a bit later in life – the last 30 years or so – because my father was not enamored of cats, probably because he didn't understand them! I've trained dogs for competitive obedience and earned titles, but after working at an animal shelter, I focused more on training and behavior modification that helped people and dogs live together better.

As of this writing, our Irish setter Coral, is at the heart of the life Dan and I share. We still miss our last cat, our wonderful male orange tabby named Buffett (do you see a theme here? Yes I've been a Parrothead since 1987!). There is no doubt another cat is in our future, when our lifestyle permits.

Our Websites

AnimalBehaviorAssociates.com

BehaviorEducationNetwork.com

CatBehaviorHelp.com

HelpingFido.com

HelpingKitty.com

PetProBehaviorGuide.com

PetProNews.com

PetProWebinars.com

PreparingFido.com

SensibleDogTraining.com

TerribleDogTrainingMistakes.com

Introduction

Welcome to *12 Terrible Dog Training Mistakes Owners Make That Ruin Their Dog's Behavior...and How to Avoid Them*. Almost every single dog owner I've worked with in the past 25+ years has made at least one of these mistakes. Most have made 4 or 5, and many have made them all. I made a few of them with my own dogs when I was first starting out in the dog training field. You'll read about some of my mistakes in this book. Back in the late 1970s and early 1980s, when I started, what we now know are mistakes, were accepted practice and "state of the art" in those days. It's inexcusable that people who call themselves professionals in the field today haven't moved past what the state of knowledge was back then.

It's time for you to discover these mistakes and get past them – something even some professionals have either been unable to, or refuse to do.

These mistakes are real. If you're making even a few of them, it can impact your relationship with your dog and your training success big time. I've had many trainers and behavior consultants I work with ask me for a book like this. They want one reference for their clients that explains rationally and scientifically why the mistakes they see dog owners making ARE mistakes. So to all those who've asked me — if this helps you make one dog and one dog owner's life better, then it's a good book!

What We'll Cover

We're going to talk about the biggest mistakes dog owners make that sabotage both their training success and their relationships with their dogs. Some of these are "sacred cows" in the dog training world, and questioning them brings the wrath of trainers who have long held to these ideas. But I've seen the negative effects on dogs, on their owners, and on family relationships from making these mistakes. You'll discover what the mistakes are, why they are so destructive, and how you can avoid making them. I'll also tell you about many other resources from both me and other professionals I trust, that will help you accomplish your behavior and training goals with your dog.

Biggest Dog Training Mistake?

The biggest training mistakes people make with their dogs revolve around trying to see the dog either as a wolf or as a person. From believing dominance and being "alpha" forms the foundation of good relationship with dogs, to thinking dogs know right from wrong and act guilty when they break the rules, it is not understanding dogs as dogs that most often causes people and dogs to be at odds with each other.

Have you been told dogs are "denning animals" and therefore it's easy for them to acclimate to crates? I've seen dogs that have injured themselves trying to escape from their crates. Been told you can reward your dog's fear? Did you know research from more than 20 years ago would beg to differ?

Think you're good at "reading" your dog? You may fall into that group of dog owners who don't readily recognize signs of fear and anxiety and are even paying attention to different bodily features from the ones professionals do.

Those are just a few of the 12 terrible dog training mistakes you'll discover in this book.

Why Correcting These Mistakes is Important

Research into the cognitive abilities of dogs and how their behavior is impacted by aspects of our relationships with them, has exploded in the past 5 to 10 years. Yet too many people who consider themselves to be professionals are stuck in the "you can't play 'tug of war' with your dog" (it's not a war, it's only a game and research has shown it bears no relationship to the development of aggression problems) or "support the alpha dog's dominance" (yep, that's what we want – a dog that will attack if he can't be king of the hill!) over-simplified model of canine social relationships. And they are foisting that sort of out dated information on you – the unsuspecting, trying to do your best, dog owner. You should be outraged – I am!

There are no licensing requirements for dog trainers, behaviorists or non-degreed behavior consultants. (Even though it's not a protected term, in this book I reserve the term "behaviorist" to apply to *only* those people who have a graduate degree in a behavioral science or to veterinarians who have completed a behavior residency, although this does not require a graduate behavioral degree.) Because there are no industry-wide educational, professional, or licensing standards for those of us in this field, it's easy for people to "make up" information about dog behavior and training practices that either has no basis in behavioral science or there is evidence that refutes the "made up stuff". This accounts for a portion of the 12 terrible mistakes.

What has also exploded in the past few years are the certifications dog trainers can earn. It truly has become an alphabet soup and in some ways just adds to the confusion in the field. However, with a few rare exceptions (and several popular media stars are NOT included in my exceptions list) I would recommend you be VERY cautious of trusting anyone who holds no behavior or training credentials at all to work with your dog. However, I've seen even credentialed people tumble to some of the mistakes I explain in this book. As a bonus chapter in this book, I've given you guidelines and criteria to help you choose a behavior or training professional as well as explaining what some of the credentials are.

What Knowing About the Mistakes Means To You

The dog owners I work with adore their dogs, but are unhappy about some facet of their dog's behavior, are frustrated because they haven't gotten the results they wanted, and are worried they aren't taking the right approach when it comes to training. I've had people call me almost in tears because they are so confused. They've received conflicting information from a variety of people – trainers, veterinarians, behavior consultants, family friends and others, and they really do not know what to do about their dog's behavior. People tell me they "are at the end of the rope", they've "tried everything", or their dog just doesn't seem to "get it".

Although I can't tell you precisely what you and your dog need, I can tell you that one or more of these mistakes is likely part of the reason you are currently "stuck". You will at least need to correct these mistakes to get "unstuck".

Bad Things Can Come From Making These Mistakes

Years ago, I was involved in a lawsuit in which a dog trainer was charged with cruelty to animals for the type of discipline he delivered to a dog he was trying to "train". His technique involved swinging the dog around his head on a choke chain and leash. Later veterinary examination revealed the dog had been blinded due to lack of oxygen to her brain. Now while that is without a doubt an extreme example, and obviously something anyone with half a brain would NEVER even contemplate doing to a dog, there are still people out there who are using harsh and dangerous procedures in the name of what they call "training".

Some training mistakes don't cause physical harm, but they do cause behavioral harm. Harm can come from making a behavior problem worse, creating other problems, and from failing to change a behavior that could be modified with the right techniques. Some of these mistakes cause harm by having a negative impact on your dog's welfare. And like traumatic events we as individuals may have experienced, we aren't always aware of the ramifications until later.

Some of the 12 mistakes undermine other good things you may be doing as you work with your dog. In some cases, this is sufficient to render the good things ineffective, and even cause you to give up or to conclude a particular technique doesn't work.

That's yet another reason why you'll want to read this book. You may be doing many things RIGHT, but because of one or two mistakes, it's all coming out wrong.

How This Book Is Different

Most books about dog training aimed at dog owners focus on specific methods and "how tos". Some of these books are great, some are terrible. None of them talk about the 12 terrible dog training mistakes, why they are mistakes, explain the damage the mistakes can cause, and back up the "whys" with scientific information.

I've already told you about the lack of consistency and agreement in the dog training and behavior world. Not only is a good portion of what you read about dog behavior mired in myths and misconceptions and sacred cow mentality, but it's sometimes impossible for you to tell the difference between good information and bad advice.

You don't need any more rhetoric that usually comes from the extremes in any field, including that of dog training and behavior. You need a book that connects behavioral science to practical dos and don'ts when it comes to your dog's behavior. That's exactly what this book does. And I'm not afraid to take the "politically incorrect" path in a few chapters, because the politically correct one doesn't always have science on its side.

So let's stop wasting time and let me tell you about the 12 terrible dog training mistakes and how can avoid them.

Chapter One: We Don't Need no Stinkin' Alpha!

The Mistake: Basing your relationship with your dog on being the "pack leader" or the "alpha".

For years, dog owners have been told that the best, and according to some, the *only* way to have a well behaved dog is to be your dog's "pack leader". The basis for this so-called "pack theory" model of dog behavior is that dogs are still wolves at heart. And that because all members of a wolf pack supposedly obey, give into, and acquiesce to the 'pack leader" or "alpha male", your dog should do the same toward you.

In order to acquire and maintain your "dominant status", this model goes on to say, certain rules must be followed. The rules vary among individual advocates of this model, but often include many of the following:

- Your dog should never be allowed to go ahead of you on walks
- Your dog should never go through doors before you
- Never feed your dog before the family eats
- Do not allow your dog on the bed or the furniture
- Don't play tug with your dog

- Never respond to your dog's attempts to initiate play, to ask for attention or to be petted

Some beliefs about how to establish "dominance" are quite bizarre. They include following your dog around the yard, urinating over areas he marked; spitting in your dog's food so your dog knows you control the food; never stepping over your dog but instead making him move out of your way; and randomly pushing your dog off his bed and sitting in it yourself so your dog knows everything belongs to you.

According to this model, for both dogs and wolves, social status is everything. Dogs are constantly finding ways to climb the social ladder, and if you aren't consistent and vigilant with these rules, your dog will begin to take charge, do whatever he wants, not do what he's told, and attempt to control you through threats and aggression.

Because status is everything, this model has to frame all misbehavior in terms of a problem in the dominance hierarchy. Your dog doesn't listen to you because you aren't a strong pack leader. Your dog soils in the house because he's trying to dominate you. Your dog eats his own feces because he knows you don't want him to and by doing it anyway he's showing you who's boss. Your dog growls at your baby because the baby isn't dominant over him. Your dog barks too much because you haven't established yourself as leader so it's his job to alert you to trouble. Your dog pulls to be ahead on walks because by being ahead of you he's showing you he's the "alpha".

Why This "Pack Leader" Model Is a Mistake

Subscribing to the "dominance model" will waste your time, cause you to focus on – and even create - conflict with your dog, prevent you from enjoying your dog, won't help you have a well behaved dog, and if followed to the extreme, will cause physical and behavioral harm to your dog. It completely flies in the face of what we know scientifically about dog, and also wolf, social behavior.

It's so outdated and disconnected from our knowledge about dogs, it's sort of like still believing, as did the early philosophers, that nonhuman animals are nothing more than machines, without emotions, or the ability to think or reason.

What Does "Being Alpha" Really Mean?

The human-as-pack-leader model of the ideal dog-human relationship is wrong for so many reasons, I could write the entire book on this one mistake. Let's first look at the basic premise: the wolf pack is organized around an "alpha" male and female, and all other pack members defer to them. Alpha status is supposedly gained through fights, conflicts, and winning or besting your opponents that challenge your "alpha" status.

Perhaps the clearest explanation for why this description of a wolf pack is wrong comes from wildlife biologist Dr. David Mech, who has studied wolves in the wild for close to 40 years (as compared the vast majority of dog trainers and others subscribing to this model who have never seen wolves in the wild, much less spent hundreds of hours observing them), and who is partially responsible for the "alpha" terminology.

Dr. Mech used the term "alpha" to mean nothing more than the breeding pair of wolves in a pack. Further, rather than members of a wolf pack being in a constant struggle for status among the pack, he likens a pack to a family. In a family, members cooperate with one another to survive, and parents and older siblings show youngsters the ways of the world. The parents - the "alphas" – aren't constantly monitoring pack members' behaviors, to make sure everybody is following the "rules", which is what the myths about wolf behavior would have you believe.

In fact, wolves have a large repertoire of behaviors whose sole purpose is to avoid conflict and settle disputes before they can escalate into fights that could injure pack members. Use the link at the end of this chapter to hear

Dr. Mech himself tell you about the problems with the idea of "alpha" and what it means in a group of wolves.

Being "Dominant" Is the Same as Having Control Over Your Dog

This is a fallacy. Training is what gives you the control you seek. Training mistakes are common, and we'll discuss a number of them in this book. If your dog doesn't come when he's called, it's not because you aren't the "pack leader", but because there has been a breakdown in how you've trained him to come. And it's unrealistic to expect any dog to come when called 100% of the time. There will always be high-level distractions that no amount of training can overcome.

For our field-bred Irish setter Coral, birds take precedence over everything else, even though she's never been trained for hunting. Coral will always come back to us after she flushes a bird, but calling her away from a bird she's stalking when she's off leash is next to impossible.

On the other hand, social hierarchies - or "dominance hierarchies" – come about as the result of direct competitions over resources. The individual that wins such a competition gets first access to whatever the competition is about, and is said to be in the dominant role. This role is only relevant to the one individual and that specific resource. Roles change depending on who is competing and what the resource is. "Dominance" is only a description of a relationship, and "dominant" describes a role in a relationship. Dominance is not an individual characteristic of a dog, but merely a description of a relationship.

Dogs Aren't Competing With Us

When it comes to our relationships with our dogs, the big mistake is assuming that for dogs everything is about competition. In the "dominance model", who is ahead on walks is somehow related to social status.

Stop and think for a moment. Being in front of you on a walk has nothing to do with competition. Why does your dog get ahead of you on a walk?

First, he can likely move faster than you. Second, he is motivated to get to the next bush to sniff and pee on, while you may just have a leisurely stroll in mind. Third, if your dog was trying to "be dominant" by being ahead, what would he do if you caught up and tried to pass him? The "dominance model" would predict he'd growl at you and warn you to stay back behind him. Have you EVER seen a dog do that? Can you even imagine a dog that would? Coral would be ecstatic if I would catch up with her, so we could move faster! I'm betting your dog feels the same way.

The same sort of logic and alternative explanations exist for every situation in the "rules" list above.

- Your dog should never go through doors before you – It's not a competition, your dog is just more motivated and capable of moving faster.
- Never feed your dog before the family eats – This stems from the mistaken idea that the "alpha" eats first. Not only is that incorrect, but it's also incorrectly assuming a direct competition exists between you and your dog for food. When your dog eats at 5pm and your family eats at 7pm, there is no direct competition.
- Do not allow your dog on the bed or the furniture – Social animals like dogs and wolves often sleep curled up together. This actually contributes to group cohesiveness and has nothing to do with social status.
- Don't play " tug of war" with your dog – Rather than a competition or a war, tug is a game in which both participants must cooperate in order for the game to continue. Watch the dog that yanks the toy out of another's mouth. Instead of trying to possess it, he'll offer it back to his play partner so the game can continue.

- Never respond to your dog's attempts to initiate play, to ask for attention or to be petted – There is just simply no basis for this rule. Dogs and wolves have complex social behaviors designed for communication. The real task is to teach your dog how to ask for what he wants. Barking in your face may not be the answer, but sitting quietly in front of you may be just the ticket, and is something you can easily teach. Lack of control over the environment, and not having a way to get needs met is a huge source of stress and anxiety for any animal. If you were to follow this "rule" with your dog, you'd be creating a cruel environment that strips away the very affectionate and playful behaviors we love the most about our dogs.

The Reasons People Easily Accept the Pack Leader Model

Most experts in dog behavior have speculated long and hard about why the "dominance" mythology has existed for so long, even when science tells us it is so wrong and so much harm has come to dogs as the result of it. I think there are three primary reasons.

Control and Dominance Are Different. First, all of us, to one degree or another, want control over our dogs. We want them to come when called, not relieve themselves in the house or dig holes in our yard, and generally respond when we tell them to do, or not do, something. The dog training literature has equated having control with being "dominant", and it's also a natural tendency for most people to do the same. We've already talked about why equating control with dominance is faulty thinking.

People Don't Like Complexity. Second, it's human nature to want to simplify complex ideas. Relationships are complex. Think about the complexity of being a parent, a spouse, a partner, or a sibling.

Relationships with our dogs are no exception. Simplifying the complexities of a relationship between two species into one supposedly simple rule – be the pack leader – means that as dog owners, we really don't have to invest the effort to learn much about what makes dogs tick. On the surface, it takes the pressure off of us to figure out how our dogs learn best, what they need, how they are feeling and thinking, and what we have to do to create a quality life for these wonderful creatures who share the most intimate part of our lives.

The recent research into the cognitive abilities of dogs provides further evidence that the simple-minded idea of human as harsh dictator isn't good for us, our dogs, or our relationship with them.

Third, until relatively recently behavior scientists and dog trainers didn't communicate much. So the dominance mythology developed unchecked by what behavior scientists have long known about social hierarchies and about wolf and dog behavior. And the mythology was given a big boost in recent years by a charismatic, self-proclaimed expert connected to a deep-pocketed marketing machine who in reality knows nothing about the science of dog behavior, and fabricated information as he went along. Now that scientists and trainers are communicating more, the claims that dogs must be ruled with a heavy hand, denied privileges, and never allowed to make any choices about their own behavior just collapse under the weight of evidence to the contrary.

What To Do Instead: How To Have A Good Relationship and a Well-Mannered Dog

There is no simple formula to replace the "pack leader" myth. Think of your relationship with your dog as part best friend, part parent, and part sibling. The characteristics of those relationships include the following:

- Friends like doing a lot of the same things, and enjoy playing and spending time together.

- There are disagreements and conflicts in the relationship, but each individual cares enough about the other to make up and forgive. (Dogs forgive us far easier than we forgive them.)
- Parents set reasonable and fair limits on behavior and help children follow them by teaching and guiding much more than disciplining.
- Each knows what the other likes and doesn't like, and tries to accommodate those preferences.
- There is shared communication. It's relatively easy to tell when the other is upset, or something is wrong. Each knows the other's unique quirks or subtle indications about what the other is likely thinking or feeling.
- Parents want the best for their children, and do whatever they can to help them reach their full potential.

Print out this list, to remind you of how much a good relationship with your dog resembles a good relationship with other people who are important in your life.

For many people, dropping the "pack leader" idea brings a sigh of relief. I can't tell you how many times people have regretfully told me how guilty they feel because they haven't been a good "alpha", or been able to be a "pack leader" and therefore caused all their dog's problems. And these are usually the people who are the most committed to their dogs and their well-being. When they learn they can have a great dog and not have to worry about being the "pack leader" they are thrilled. Just as you should be now.

My Best Advice

If you've been a stickler for the "dominance rules" with your dog, and relate to your dog as an inflexible "pack leader" your dog was afraid to offend, and you still aren't having the relationship with your dog that you want, letting go of these myths may be the single most important thing you can do to improve your relationship. The remaining eleven mistakes will give you more information about what to do instead that will transform your relationship with your dog.

For more in-depth coverage of the dangers that the "dominance" model of relationships presents I recommend our DVD "The Dangers of Dominance". This is a lecture I've given to both lay and professional groups in three countries, and you can hear it from your own living room.

Summary

I've lived with dogs since I was 5 years old. All my dogs since childhood have slept on the bed, been allowed to walk ahead of me at least some, and in Coral's case, all of the time on walks, usually been fed before my family sat down to breakfast or dinner, played tug games with me, stood over and licked me while I'm on the floor exercising (a supposedly "dominant" behavior), and violated many of the other rules laid down by the pack leader advocates.

So although I've violated every single "pack leader rule", not a single one of my dogs has ever growled at me or bitten me or anyone else; I've never had to relinquish a dog because of behavior problems; I've been able to handle them easily, trim their nails, and brush their teeth; they come when called (allowing for Coral's rule of coming when the bird is gone!); I take food and toys away from them, and aside from a bit of persistent digging (Coral likes to bury her dog cookies) and occasional excessive barking (one Dalmatian), their behavior and my relationship with them has been nothing but a source of joy, and has enriched my life in more ways than I can count.

Are you ready to learn more about how I, and the thousands of dog owners I've helped, avoided the other eleven terrible dog training mistakes? If so, let's move on to Mistake Number Two.

Resources Mentioned in this Chapter

Interview with Dr. David Mech

http://www.youtube.com/watch?v=tNtFgdwTsbU

The Dangers of Dominance DVD

http://animalbehaviorassociates.com/dvd-dangersofdominance.htm

Links to all the resources mentioned in this chapter can also be found at www.TerribleDogTrainingMistakes.com

The links to all of the references and resources listed in this book can also be accessed from www.TerribleDogTrainingMistakes.com

Chapter Two: Stay Calm and Carry On

The Mistake: Thinking that if you pay attention to or try to reassure your dog when she's fearful you are "reinforcing" her fear.

Of all the myths and misconceptions that have surrounded dog behavior and training for a very long time, perhaps one of the most persistent is the claim that it is possible to reinforce an animal's fear by paying attention to him or trying to reassure him. This was certainly a belief some of my first mentors indoctrinated me with close to thirty years ago. It's been one of the "sacred cows" of dog training for longer than that. But it's really one of the 12 terrible dog training mistakes.

If it were true that reassuring, comforting or paying attention to your dog while he's fearful "reinforces" his fear, then one or both of the following MUST be happening:

1. Your dog can learn to make a conscious decision to show fearful behaviors - act afraid - even if he isn't, because he's learned that's a good way to get attention. This means your dog is capable of faking an emotional reaction.

2. If you can actually "reinforce fear" that means you can make your dog more fearful by paying attention to him. That's what reinforcement does – encourages behavior. So the "reinforcing fear" claim means you are actually enhancing your dog's feelings of fear when you pay attention to him.

Why This Is a Mistake

Let's examine each of these underlying processes. First, let's talk about the nature of fear. Fear has emotional, behavioral, and physiological components. When we feel afraid, we act afraid, and our physiology changes (our heart rate and respiratory rate increase, for example) in response to the chemicals released into our bloodstream when we are confronted with something that scares us.

Each of these expressions of fear influences the other. If our heart rate slows, and we breathe more deeply and slowly, this will often result in decreasing our feelings of fear, and in turn our behavior changes as well.

Humans can choose to act afraid, even when they really aren't. Think of a teenaged girl (sorry I'm being a bit sexist) who screams and acts like a "drama queen" in response to some trivial startling event. Or better yet, think about all the fantastic actors we watch on the big screen and on television who without a doubt make us believe they are terrified in the scenes they are in, yet we know it's all a fantasy.

Take that example one step further. Sometimes you'll see canine actors in commercials who've been trained to lie down, hide their heads, or put a paw over their eyes to make us think they are ashamed or frightened. Yet it's easy to tell, without a doubt, that these are trained behaviors, and the dogs aren't fearful at all.

That's because dogs don't pretend. Their behaviors match their emotional state. (People aren't always good at being aware of the behaviors that indicate fear, stress, or anxiety, but that's the topic for Mistake Number 9. Your dog is not going show observable signs of fear - panting, shaking, quivering, pacing, drooling or hiding - unless he is feeling afraid.

Can you imagine your dog showing all those behaviors, but "inside", emotionally, he's quite calm knowing he's manipulating you to get attention? Wouldn't it just be easier to walk up to you and bark or paw at you, or push his head under your hand if he wants to be petted? When you think of it logically, "faking" all those fearful behaviors just to get a little attention would be a waste of effort, when your dog can accomplish the same goal so much easier with other behaviors.

That leads us to the second way of looking at this claim. If fear is being "reinforced", that means when you talk soothingly to your dog, pet him, or hold him close when he's afraid you are intensifying his feelings of fear. Does that make any sense to you?

Many dogs seek out contact from their owners during a thunderstorm. Why would a dog want to be near someone whose presence only makes him more afraid?

The Reasons Why This Myth Persists

The belief that we can "reinforce fear" in our dogs, likely persists because of how people behave. We all know individuals with a "martyr" mentality who will act fearful and helpless just to get attention and have others take care of them.

This doesn't seem to be true for animals. They don't pretend. If they don't feel afraid, they don't act afraid. When their emotional state changes, so do their behaviors.

Do you believe that when parents comfort a child who's woken up from a bad dream, or has become frightened by watching a scary movie, that their actions are making him feel more fearful? I would hope not.

A Personal Example

Let me tell you about our dog Coral. Coral is a field-bred Irish setter, and a very gentle dog. She had her share of health challenges when she was young including eye surgery, and two very complicated and painful abdominal surgeries. Consequently, she becomes very anxious and fearful when we take her to the veterinarian, even for just routine check-ups.

How do we know she's afraid? She pants, she paces, and she shakes. She paws at the door to leave. We can feel her heart beating much faster than normal.

We know Coral will never be completely relaxed and calm while at the veterinary clinic. But we've found we can reduce her stress and calm her down to some degree by doing things we know she likes.

Coral loves to have the back of her ears rubbed. She also likes it when we whisper in her ear. We aren't making this up. When we sit on the floor or couch with Coral at home, she'll often come up and position herself so that the side of her face is close to ours. She'll put her front paws on our thighs, and move close to our faces. We literally talk to her in a whisper, with our mouths right up against her ear.

How do we know she likes this? First because she willingly places her body in the positions I described. Second, if we stop whispering or stop rubbing her ears, she'll move closer or do something (like pawing at us) to encourage us to continue.

If we were "rewarding" Coral's fear at the veterinary clinic by giving her ear rubs and whispering to her, her signs of fear would worsen. This doesn't happen. When we rub her ears and "do whispers", Coral's panting decreases, her heart rate slows, and she stops shaking. She's not completely relaxed, but it's clear she is less distressed.

So rather than making Coral more fearful, or intensifying her signs of fear, just the opposite occurs.

Could Coral learn to pant, shake, and pace in settings other than the veterinary clinic in order to get us to rub her ears? Theoretically perhaps, but that's a BIG learning task. It requires considerable energy and effort to get that worked up just to get petted! Coral doesn't have to "fake" or pretend to be afraid just to get attention. She has many other behaviors she can show to get us to rub her ears and "do whispers" that routinely work for her. She's not showing these behaviors at the veterinarian's to get attention, but because she is afraid.

What To Do When Your Dog is Afraid

So, if your dog is afraid of say thunder, you now know that holding your pet and calmly stroking her is not making her more fearful. Instead, like with Coral, reassuring her can have a beneficial effect. If paying attention to your dog helps her stay calm and carry on, then do whatever works!

An alternative way to help calm your dog is to attempt to engage her in another behavior. This will not work for Coral, because her fear is too intense. But my first setter, Blaze, loved to fetch a ball. Blaze was also afraid of thunder. If the thunder was far away, or not too loud, I could often distract her by playing fetch with her. If the thunder got too loud, Blaze's fear increased to the point she was no longer interested in playing ball. At that point just allowing her to lie next to me while I petted her was most successful in managing her thunder phobia.

What Science Has to Say

Back in the 1940s, behavioral researchers conditioned rats to jump to the other side of their enclosure in order to avoid a shock that followed a buzzer. In the next phase of training, the researchers changed the sequence so that cheese followed the buzzer and the shock was discontinued.

The cheese followed the buzzer, even as the rats jumped to the other side. Similar to the attention you give your dog when she's afraid, if the cheese rewards the fear-motivated jumping, then jumping should increase, right? That's what would happen if you believe the jumping behavior (and therefore the fear) was reinforced by the cheese.

Just the opposite occurred. The rats' fear decreased, the jumping stopped and they began to eat the cheese. This is an example of classical conditioning changing behavior by changing an emotional state. Just as you have the potential to change your dog's emotional state, and therefore decrease her fear, the cheese changed what the rats anticipated. When that changed, their fear-motivated jumping stopped. Rather than cheese rewarding fear (and therefore jumping), it decreased both.

More Resources

If you want more detailed plans about how to help your fearful dog, we have a number of resources for you:

Geared toward the professional, our comprehensive program "Using Counter Conditioning and Desensitization Techniques Effectively" is the DVD of our two session webinar course. Also included are detailed notes, and an audio CD of multiple Q&A sessions from course participants.

Our webinar course "Understanding and Helping the Fearful Animal" will help you prevent, manage, and resolve fear related problems.

My Best Advice

It's hard to watch someone we love be afraid and terrified. It's natural to want to reach out and comfort our loved ones, and calm their fears. While comforting your dog won't fix or change your dog's fearful reaction, it may help reduce her fear in the moment. It's a shame that dog owners have been told for years they could make fear worse by merely doing what comes naturally.

If being close to you decreases your dog's fear, don't hesitate to reassure her. Then get professional help to reduce your dog's fearful reactions long term. You may need short-term anti-anxiety medication prescribed by your veterinarian, along with working with a degreed and certified behaviorist, non-degreed behavior consultant, or dog trainer who is very knowledgeable about dog behavior and learning. Ask the people you are considering working with if they believe fear can be rewarded. Don't work with the ones who answer yes.

Summary

In this chapter I gave you real life, practical, and personal examples of why refusing to pay attention to your dog when she's fearful is a mistake. And I gave you just one example of the body of scientific evidence showing that when emotional states govern behavior, influencing the emotional state is a highly effective way to change voluntary behaviors.

Rewarding fear is just one of many examples of "sacred cows" in the dog training world. There are so many of these, we in fact have done two webinar courses on sacred cows. You'll find them both at PetProWebinars.com.

In the next chapter, we'll take up another sacred cow – that of confining your dog in a crate.

Resources Mentioned in This Chapter

The Sacred Cows of Dog Training

http://petprowebinars.com/courses-by-instructor/kathy-sdaos-classes/sacred-cows-of-dog-training-part-2/

Understanding and Helping the Fearful Animal

http://petprowebinars.com/courses-by-instructor/understanding-and-helping-fearful-animals/

Using Counter Conditioning and Desensitization Techniques Effectively

http://animalbehaviorassociates.com/mp3-counter-conditioning.htm

Links to all the resources mentioned in this chapter can also be found at www.TerribleDogTrainingMistakes.com

The links to all of the references and resources listed in this book can also be accessed from www.TerribleDogTrainingMistakes.com

Chapter Three: This Den Just Isn't My Thing

The Mistake: Assuming dogs are "denning" animals and will easily accept being crated. Believing this can lead to also believing it's acceptable to keep your dog confined in a crate most days.

At one point or another, it's likely you've probably been advised by someone to confine your dog in a crate. Crate confinement is often recommended as an aid in housetraining a puppy, or even an older dog because dogs supposedly don't like to soil their dens. If your dog is showing unwanted behavior when left alone – usually being destructive or soiling – confining him in a crate may have been the first recommendation you received. Crates are also used as a safe way to restrain a dog while traveling in the car, and of course the airlines require dogs be crated.

If you ask what size of crate you should get, the answer usually is something similar to: "the crate should be just big enough to allow your dog to stand up and turn around. Anything bigger and there would be enough room for your dog to relieve himself in one end, and have a clean area at the other". If a dog soils in the crate, often people are told to get a smaller crate, or make the existing crate smaller by blocking off the dog's access to part of it.

I've talked to dog owners who were crating their dogs seven days a week, sometimes as long as 8 to 10 hours each day while they were away at work. The dogs were also sleeping in the crate at night. This left maybe 4 or at most 5 hours of free time in the evenings and more on the weekends or the owners' days off. When I've asked people their reasons for this sort of confinement schedule, their answers are either the dog gets into trouble if left free in the house, OR they crated their dog to housetrain him as a puppy and just never got out of the habit.

The reasoning behind why proponents of crating say dogs don't mind being crated is that dogs are "denning" animals. As such, they supposedly are inherently adapted to, and even enjoy, spending time in small, confined spaces.

Why Crating Can Be a Mistake

First let's list all the mistakes in this view of the use of crates, and then I'll explain why they are mistakes:

1. Dogs don't mind being confined because they are denning animals

2. If your dog soils the crate, make it smaller

3. If your dog misbehaves when left alone the first, and best, solution is to crate him.

Dogs as Denning Animals

What does this really mean? It's true that most wild canids use dens for whelping and raising puppies. Adult wolves, and the pups as they mature and become mobile, come and go from their dens as they please. When crated and left alone, a crate is used as forced confinement and is not at all analogous to the free access of a den. Some dogs choose to go into their crates when the door is open, as they find it a protected place to rest. That's quite different from being confined there for long hours, particularly when confinement happens most often when the dog is left alone. For dogs that are consistently crated when left alone, confinement becomes synonymous with social isolation.

Second, dens are used most often in the wild when the pups are small. As the pups mature, they and their parents spend less time in the den. They are not used routinely or consistently throughout the year. Compare this to a crate which may be used daily for the life of the dog. Adult wild canids do not spend the majority of their days in the den, but a dog that is crated daily for hours sure does.

Third, wild pups are born in the den, making this a familiar place for them from birth. Many dogs are not exposed to a crate until they are adults, and if not properly acclimated, can find a crate (or other types of confinement) quite anxiety-producing. In fact, crate confinement as an attempt to manage soiling or destructive problems that are fear-motivated almost always results in the dog panicking even more.

Excessive crating means a dog can't possibly get his needs met for exercise, mental stimulation, social contact, and play.

Dogs Don't Like To Soil Their "Dens" / Crates

This is the underlying assumption behind using a crate for housetraining. What the scientific literature on behavioral development in the dog actually says is that around 3-4 weeks of age, puppies are more able to move around independently and can relieve themselves without help from mom. With the development of these two abilities, puppies naturally tend to move away from the whelping or resting area when the need to relieve themselves arises.

Being confined doesn't help a puppy or dog learn to control his bladder and bowels. That happens through normal, physiological processes. The benefit to using a crate as part of a housetraining protocol is to prevent the dog from soiling inside when someone isn't home to supervise him and let him outside at regular intervals. Confinement doesn't somehow magically teach bladder and bowel control.

If the puppy is confined too long, he will need to relieve himself. That's not a good situation. But if a last-minute event prevents an owner from getting home in time to let the puppy out, the crate *should* be large enough for the puppy to have an elimination area away from his resting area. Not providing for this goes against the puppy's natural tendencies. That just makes housetraining harder. Puppies raised in puppy mills who have no choice but to relieve themselves in the same areas they sleep are virtually impossible to housetrain because their natural tendencies have been overridden by their environment.

Confinement for long hours without the ability to relieve himself is not good for any dog. I've had clients tell me their dogs can "hold it" for a 10-hour work day. Maybe the dog can, but I'll wager he's not comfortable doing it. Dogs need potty breaks that meet their biological and behavioral needs.

Make the Crate Smaller

I see red when I hear this recommendation. If a dog is soiling the crate SOMETHING IS WRONG. And the answer is DEFINITELY NOT to make the crate smaller OR to deprive the dog of water while he's crated. Some of these "make the crate smaller" recommendations result in dogs being confined in smaller spaces and for longer time periods than is allowed by federal law for dogs in research facilities!

 Instead, the first step is to find out what's wrong. It's likely one of four problems:

1. The dog is being confined for longer than he can control his bladder or bowels.

2. The dog didn't have a chance to relieve himself immediately before being crated.

3. The dog is afraid or panicked in the crate, which is causing the soiling.

4. The dog is ill (perhaps a bladder infection or any one of a laundry list of possible reasons) and needs to be evaluated by a veterinarian.

Crating to Manage or Prevent Problem Behavior

The most common reason I see owners crating their dogs when left alone is because the dog is soiling in the house or being destructive. The majority of these problems are fear-motivated, with the most common fears being separation anxiety and noise phobias.

Confinement of a dog that is already fearful is a recipe for disaster, as this will only increase the dog's panic. I've seen dogs that have broken their teeth, torn up their paws, scratched their faces, and bloodied themselves in other ways trying to get out of a crate. I wish I'd taken pictures of the most memorable cases I saw.

In one, when I walked up to the house, sitting on the front porch was a metal crate so mangled it looked like King Kong had tried to crush it. In reality a large white shepherd was responsible, trying to escape while panicking when left alone during a thunder storm.

The second most unforgettable case was seeing the crate wrapped with two metal chains and two padlocks. The dog apparently had been able to work the latch on the door free, so rather than realizing their dog was utterly terrorized in the crate, the owners' response had been to try to create a prison from which the dog could not escape.

The Right Ways to Use a Crate

Now that I've pointed out the mistakes made trying to make a crate analogous to a den and the problems caused by overuse of crates, let me say I am not completely against the use of crates. A crate can be a good training and short-term management option if the guidelines below are followed:

1. The dog must be gradually acclimated to a crate using a detailed crate training protocol.

2. The crate must be large enough for the dog to lay down fully extended and to be able to lay on his side, legs comfortably straight

3. The dog's behavior when first left alone in the crate must be monitored (using video if necessary)

4. Owners must recognize when a crate is not appropriate for their dog, based on the dog's behavior. Not all dogs can be successfully acclimated to a crate.

5. The crate should only be a short-term management or safety tool. Crate confinement should not be a routine way of life for dogs. Owners need to transition dogs to being left free in the house, and also resolve whatever problem prompted the consistent use of a crate in the first place.

Not following these guidelines compromises a dog's welfare, and also increases the risk of the dog not staying in the home. One study found that dogs who were consistently confined in crates or left alone in the backyard during the day, were at greater risk of surrender to animal shelters than those who had access to the house*

Crate Training Resources

There are many good crate training protocols as well as some that aren't so good. A good one is **"Crate Training the Right Way"** a DVD that is available at your local PetSmart® store. My husband Dr. Dan Estep and I wrote the script for this program and also assisted in its production.

Our book **"Raising a Behaviorally Healthy Puppy"** also contains a crate training protocol, as well as training plans for housetraining, preventing chewing, appropriate socialization and more. You can purchase this book at http://terribledogtrainingmistakes.com/resources/puppy-book/

Online, try the ASPCA's crate training protocol, although I'd recommend disregarding their sizing recommendations and instead opt for a crate sufficiently large to give your dog a bit of moving-around room. We used a crate to aid in housetraining our Irish setter Coral that was large enough for an adult setter. So Coral had more than enough room to use one end of the crate for elimination, but she never did. If a healthy puppy is resorting to soiling while confined then she's being confined for too long OR she hasn't been properly acclimated to the crate and is frightened. Period

If you'd like me to send you my crate training protocol go to www.SensibleDogTraining.com/crate-training, and enter your name and email and I'll be happy to do so.

Crate Alternatives

A crate is probably the safest way for a dog to ride in the car. Our Coral however, like some dogs, gets carsick when riding in a crate, but is fine when sitting on the seat. So we use a harness and dog seat belt for her.

Like car travel, there are other options for restricting your dog's access to the house if this is necessary short-term. Baby gates are often good solutions, as is the simple act of just closing doors to rooms you don't want your dog to be in.

If you are housetraining, consider confining your puppy in a small area such as a laundry room, and creating a potty area using indoor pads designed for that purpose. Given that puppies tend to move away from the areas they rest and sleep when they need to relieve themselves that seems the best compromise. You can even use a small piece of artificial turf placed on top of a plastic box lid to create something that resembles the outdoor grass you want the puppy to use.

Ideas vary as to how often dogs need a break to relieve themselves. The ASPCA's website gives the following table:

8–10 weeks 30–60 minutes

11–14 weeks 1–3 hours

15–16 weeks 3–4 hours

17+ weeks 4–5 hours

I don't like having adult dogs spend more than 4 hours in a crate (unless it's a rare or unusual occurrence in an emergency), and I would lower the recommended time for dogs younger than 6 months to no more than three hours.

Finally, if you are using a crate to manage an existing soiling, destructive, or other sort of problem, it's time to resolve the problem rather than crating your dog every day.

Most dogs can be transitioned to more freedom in the house. If for some reason your dog cannot be given free access to the house, then consider some other way to restrict his access, as discussed above. A dog should not spend most of his time confined in a crate.

My Best Advice

I've lived with dogs since I was five years old. When I was growing up, we never heard of the practice of crating dogs, and neither did any of our friends and families with dogs. It wasn't until many years later when I first started competing in obedience and training dogs professionally that I was introduced to crates for dogs.

Until I went to graduate school and started reading the scientific literature on behavioral development in the dog, and became involved in the welfare of dogs maintained in facilities, I too bought into the myths about a crate being like a den.

Recommending the use of a crate for a dog used to be much more of a sacred cow in the dog training world than it is now. Asking their feelings about the use of crates is another evaluation topic you can use when interviewing people you are considering hiring to help you work with your dog.

Summary

It's easy to see why the "crate as a den" view is appealing. But once we take a look at what the research has to say about behavioral development in the dog, and what biologists and ethologists know about how dens are used in the wild, you can see where the analogy falls apart. It broke my heart to encounter dogs that spent so much time in their crates it was no wonder their behavior was crazy and uncontrollable in the evenings because they had so much pent-up energy.

In this chapter you learned how you could use a crate appropriately for short-term management and training, to avoid the pitfall of selecting a crate that is too small for your dog, the guidelines for duration of crating, the importance of following a crate training protocol to gradually acclimate your dog to crate confinement, alternatives to crates, and how to know when use of a crate is not appropriate for a dog.

I mentioned one of the concerns about excessive crating is that dogs are not getting their physical and behavioral needs met. That leads us to Mistake Number Four and the next chapter "These Paws Are Made For Walkin'". Want to guess what it's about?

*Patronek. G.J., Glickman, L.T., Beck, A. M., McCabe, G.P. and C. Ecker, 1996. Risk factors for relinquishment of dogs to an animal shelter. JAVMA 209: 572-581.

Resources Mentioned in This Chapter

Raising a Behaviorally Healthy Puppy

http://animalbehaviorassociates.com/book-raising-behaviorally-healthy-puppy.htm

The ASPCA's Crate Training Protocol

http://www.aspca.org/pet-care/virtual-pet-behaviorist/dog-behavior/weekend-crate-training

Obtain our crate training protocol at

http://www.TerribleDogTrainingMistakes.com/crate-training

The links to all of the references and resources listed in this book can also be accessed from www.TerribleDogTrainingMistakes.com

Chapter 4 These Paws Are Made for Walkin'

The Mistake: Your dog doesn't need outside walks because he has a big back yard and tons of toys.

Why This Is a Mistake

Most dogs do not self-exercise. One of my Dalmatians, Ashley, was the rare dog who did a bit of this. She'd grab a small rock from my flower bed, throw it up in the air, then pick it up, race around the yard with it, drop it, and then repeat the entire process. Most dogs need a social partner for play and obviously your dog needs you to take her for a walk.

Even though you may have a big back yard for your dog, most dogs aren't going to run around it on their own. Your dog may have a short burst of activity when she runs a squirrel up the fence, as our dog Coral does. Or if you have more than one dog, they may have several play bouts of chasing each other around the yard or tugging on a toy, but this isn't the same experience as the prolonged motion or sensory stimulation dogs get during walks.

Healthy, young and middle-aged dogs are not inherently couch potatoes. That sedentary, inactive lifestyle has become the default for too many dogs because it mimics our own. It's common knowledge that the majority of Americans are overweight, and veterinarians now also tell us that obesity is a bigger and bigger problem in both dogs and cats.

In addition to the health problems inactivity causes, you might not have thought about the behavior consequences. Let me give you a very personal and timely example.

A Personal Example

While writing this chapter I was juggling too many other commitments. When several things went wrong all at once, in the span of just a few minutes (emails wouldn't go through forcing me to rewrite them; additional deadlines were forced on me without notice, etc.) I "lost it" as we say, and my temper got the better of me. I was so agitated, not only could I not think, but I was shaking, not to mention yelling. Had I been a dog, I would probably have been growling or barking, and would have bitten the first person who got too close or tried to pet me.

What did I do? I went for a walk. The sun was shining, the palm trees were swaying gently in a light, cool breeze, puffy clouds were on the horizon, and the air smelled clean and warm. If I were a dog, there would have been even more pleasant sensory input to refocus my attention such as innumerable interesting smells and who-knows-what sounds from blocks away.

When I returned to the house, life was still far from perfect but at least I was calm enough to sit down, concentrate, and resume work on this chapter. Walks have the same calming and distracting effects on our dogs.

How Walks Help

When stress levels are high, our bodies, and our dogs' as well, release a number of chemicals that prepare us for the "fight or flight" reaction. While that's really an oversimplification of what's going on, the fact remains that physical activity helps to dissipate these chemicals, decrease our stress, and help us feel better.

Dogs thrive on activity. If you are a parent you know how children get when they've been inside for too long during bad weather. Dogs are probably even more sensitive to inactivity, but we often don't think to link some of their unwanted behaviors to the fact that they aren't getting enough exercise.

Here's just a partial list of dog behaviors and problems that could benefit from more exercise:

1. Dogs can be destructive when they have too much pent-up energy and no acceptable way to release it. They may choose to dig holes, chew on furniture, get into the trash, or turn who-knows-what into a tug or chew toy.

2. Extended barking bouts can be a way to release energy that has no other outlet. Dogs barking for this reason may seem to be barking at nothing. Even barking that initially occurs in reaction to some event may go on for much longer than needed.

3. Fear causes tension, release of some of those same 'flight or fight" chemicals, and leaves our dogs tired and exhausted. Walking is relaxing and allows dogs to release muscle tension.

4. If there is conflict among your family dogs, walking helps to release built-up tension, and *may* be a shared activity that can be the first step in helping them to get along better.

5. Your dog may have a low tolerance for your children. Kids can be annoying – they are often loud, they run around creating chaos, and they do unpredictable things like suddenly jumping off the couch and landing right next to your dog. Babies and toddlers can be quite frightening to dogs, as they invade the dog's personal space on the floor. Taking a walk provides a mini getaway for your dog and gives him a chance to relax.

6. Generally being hard to control and pestering for attention. If your dog is practically vibrating because of pent-up energy, it's hard for him to sit or lie down and hang out while you watch television. One of our Dalmatians, Ashley, had an above-average need to be active, and a low tolerance for inactivity. In her younger years, it was very difficult for her to be still for any length of time. We walked Ashley regularly, but she probably would have made a great companion for a long-distance runner who did daily runs of 5 or 6 miles. If a day went by without a walk, Ashley's annoying behaviors increased dramatically.

Hopefully, you're seeing a pattern here. Anytime a dog is frustrated, anxious, "bored", afraid, or angry, a walk can help to "let go" of those reactions and release physical and emotional tension. Don't be confused however about what I'm saying. Exercise won't resolve those problems -- specific behavior modification interventions are needed for that. But walks and other exercise can reduce the aftereffects, and perhaps raise the dog's threshold for some of those emotional responses. Another way to say it, is that with more physical activity, your dog is likely to be less "on edge", not as easily startled or frightened, and less ready for a fight. Physical activity can increase his tolerance of the things in life he has a hard time with.

Sniffing Is More Important Than You Think

Most dogs do a lot of sniffing on walks. Some dog trainer mythology may hold that you shouldn't allow your dog to stop and sniff – you should set the pace and your dog should follow you. That's more "pack leader" nonsense. Sniffing provides tremendous environmental enrichment, takes more energy than you would think, and adds immeasurably to the quality of your dog's walk.

It's hard for us to understand how important sniffing is for dogs, because it is a world of odors and olfactory stimulation that we can't share. When we took Coral through a beginning K9NoseWork® class, our instructor warned us she would be quite tired when she got home. We were dubious, but the instructor was right.

In case you aren't familiar with NoseWork®, it's an easier version of professional scent work, scaled way back from what the various types of scent detection dogs are trained to do. In Coral's class, we hid containers of treats in various places in the training room for her to sniff out and find. Each dog works alone, so it's a great activity for dogs that don't do well in other sorts of training classes because they can't get along with other dogs. Enrolling in a NoseWork®, or other scent work class, is another great option to provide your dog with more physical and mental activity.

What a Good Walk Looks Like

An enrichment walk is not an obedience or training lesson. If you want to work on training your dog to walk next to you, do it in another session. In an enrichment walk, your dog gets to have most of the say about when and where to stop to sniff. The only guideline is that he's not pulling so hard or is so out of control that it makes the walk potentially dangerous or very uncomfortable for you.

Avoid using buckle collars, choke chains, or pinch collars. Unless they are extra wide to distribute the pulling force, buckle collars typically put too pressure on the trachea, causing most dogs to gag. Choke chains are even worse in that regard. And pinch collars, because they hurt, can create aggression problems, if you yank back on the leash when your dog sees another dog or person. Plus, they take all the fun out of an enrichment walk, where your dog should be allowed to get out in front or move to either side to stop and sniff.

Opt instead for either a walking or no-pull harness. There are more and more varieties available, but I recommend the ones from Dean and Tyler (thanks to my friend, colleague, and fellow CAAB Nancy Williams from <u>Dogs</u>

With Issues who introduced me to them!) (Nancy's an Associate CAAB meaning she has a Master's degree). If you want a no-pull version, get the Universal DT No Pull Plus. If you want just a regular walking/working harness get the DT Harness which is what we use with Coral. The DT Fun Harness is another possibility. Even though she's small, Coral is quite deep-chested so we also had to add the Strap Extension.

A halter, sometimes referred to as a head collar is another possibility. While these collars used to be well thought of by most progressive trainers, they seem to have fallen somewhat into disfavor for reasons I don't fully understand. I think this is due in part because of misconceptions about how they should be fitted, and lack of instruction to owners about how to use them.

If the no-pull harness doesn't limit your dog's pulling enough for the walk to be safe and enjoyable for you, then consider a head collar, which will prevent pulling if used correctly.

I'd recommend the Snoot Loop. While it takes a bit more time to get the fit right initially, it's more comfortable for your dog. Other options include the Gentle Leader® and the Halti®.

It's imperative though that you keep the leash loose and allow your dog his sniffing time. If you need to limit the pulling, keep your leash parallel to the ground, and put some gentle but steady tension on the leash. This will turn your dog's head toward you. As soon as that happens, release the tension. You may need help from a professional trainer to get started using a head collar correctly. You might find the online Gentle Leader Instructional Video listed in the Resource Section helpful.

Walking Schedule

I'm suggesting your goal be to walk EVERY day with your dog, or as close to every day as is humanly possible, and no less than 5 times a week, weather permitting. This is in addition to any backyard or in the house play time. Playtime is great but it doesn't take the place of a walk for reasons I already explained.

If you believe either you or your dog or both are really out of shape and overweight, then start walking every other day to give you both some recovery time. Or walk every day, but for very brief periods. But if you start with less than every day, make sure you have a time schedule for when you will work up to every day.

The duration of the walk depends on your dog's needs, and your dog's and your, physical condition. We take Coral on our 45-minute, twice a week runs and she gets a walk every day of at least that long and sometimes for an hour or more. The little dogs we see frequenting our neighborhood, and owned by people older than us, are still getting several walks each day of likely 10-15 minutes each. If you're not sure what's best for your dog, ask your veterinarian what s/he would recommend, given your dog's size, age, weight and breed type.

Walking Benefits You As Well

There is a substantial, and growing, body of evidence that shows walking your dog is good for you as well. According to a Canadian study, dog ownership almost doubled the amount of time people spent walking. Not including the time spent walking their dogs, dog owners actually spent less time exercising than did nonowners, which means their walking was motivated at least in part by the needs of their dogs.

A study from the University of Missouri found that overweight participants who walked dogs for 20 minutes five days a week for a year lost an average of 14 pounds. New research from Michigan State University reports that dog owners are 34% more likely to get the recommended 150 minutes of exercise a week than are non-dog owners*.

Because walking is so beneficial for both you and your dog, there should be NO reason not to continue or start a regular walking program with your dog. You may think it's hard to fit a walk into an already busy schedule, but I'll virtually guarantee you can carve out an extra 15-20 minutes from somewhere, if you're committed. Watch one less TV program (or record it). Spend less time on the phone (not ideal, but you could complete a phone call while walking). Spend less time posting on Facebook. Get up 15 minutes earlier. There is always a way if it's important enough to you. Your dog would say it's DEFINITELY important enough to find the time.

Some people avoid walking the dog because of their dogs' behavior on walks. We've already talked about how a head collar or no-pull harness can help. If the problem is your dog's behavior when encountering another dog, you'll want to read the next chapter. In "Friend or Foe, You Just Never Know", I'll tell you how to avoid the mistake of letting your dog greet another leashed dog during walks.

My Best Advice

There is no doubt that it takes time and commitment to create a new habit. But I'll bet after a few weeks or a month, you'll come to enjoy your walking habit so much that you won't have any trouble making it a priority.

Your new habit may be easier to establish if you can find a walking partner. Perhaps you could ask a friend or neighbor to join you. Walking groups are springing up all over, often starting as Meet Ups. (www.MeetUp.com)

Summary

In this chapter I made the case for how walking can have a positive effect on a variety of behavior problems. Increasing your dog's activity levels also is good for his overall health, can have a huge impact on weight loss, and provides environmental enrichment. You discovered how important sniffing opportunities are for dogs, and the difference between an enrichment walk and a training session.

Dan and I look forward to our daily walks with Coral almost as much as she does. As of this writing, Coral is a month shy of 10 years old. We know we don't have that many more years to have the privilege of daily walks with her, and we view each one we have as a cherished gift.

References

The Canadian Dog Walking Study

Brown, S. G., and R. E. Rhodes, 2006. Relationships Among Dog Ownership and Leisure-Time Walking in

Western Canadian Adults. American Journal of Preventive Medicine 30 (2): 131-136. Read the abstract using the link below

http://www.ajpmonline.org/article/S0749-3797%2805%2900399-5/abstract

The Michigan Dog Walking Study

Reeves, M.J. et al. 2011, The Impact of Dog Walking on Leisure-Time Physical Activity: Results From a Population-Based Survey of Michigan Adults. J. of Physical Activity and Health, 8 (3): 436-444. Download the article using the link below

http://journals.humankinetics.com/jpah-pdf-articles?DocumentScreen=Detail&ccs=6412&cl=18637

Zeltzman, P. and R. A. Johnson. 2011. Walk a Hound, Lose a Pound. Purdue University Press.

Resources Mentioned in This Chapter

Dean   and   Tyler   Working   Harness
http://www.dtdogcollars.com/DT-Harness-High-quality-Nylon-Dog-Harness-p/dth6.htm

K9NoseWork
http://www.k9nosework.com/

Universal Dean and Tyler No Pull Harness

http://www.dtdogcollars.com/product-p/dthunvplus.htm

Dean and Tyler Strap Extension

http://www.dtdogcollars.com/product-p/dth6ext.htm

The Gentle Leader Instructional Video

http://www.youtube.com/watch?v=_y3sjc1yY50

The Snoot Loop

http://www.snootloop.com

The links to all of the references and resources listed in this book can also be accessed from www.TerribleDogTrainingMistakes.com

Chapter 5: Friend or Foe, You Just Never Know

The Mistake: Allowing your dog to greet other dogs when walking on leash.

So you've decided to take my advice and have embarked on your first day of regular walks with your dog. You and your dog are enjoying the outdoors, your dog is trotting along, stopping to sniff at will, and up ahead you see another dog and owner approach. Your dog's head pops up from whatever he was sniffing, and about the same time the other dog sees your dog. The approaching dog starts pulling at the leash, your dog does the same and both act as though they are long- lost friends who can't wait to see each other, even though this is their first meeting.

As you approach each other, the dogs' excitement seems to grow. They both start barking, paws skittering on the side walk as the tension on the leash causes them to lose traction as their tails wag furiously. You are anticipating a joyous encounter and a bit of play when WHAM, the other dog jumps on your dog (or vice versa) and rather than a friendly meeting, you've got two dogs growling and jumping on each other (or one dog doing that while the other tries to get the heck out of there). What you had thought was going to be a friendly greeting turns into an unpleasant and frightening encounter for both people and dogs.

This is such a common scenario that dog trainers and behaviorists have coined a special term for it – leash aggression. While some leashed greetings can go well, the problem, as the chapter title says, you just never know.

What To Do From Here

If your dog already has doggie friends that the two of you encounter on a regular basis, and the dogs do well with each other then it's probably OK to continue to allow the two of them to meet and greet (although once you read Chapter 9 you may change your mind as to whether your dog is "OK" or not). But to avoid the very real risk of having the encounter go bad, I'd recommend – as do many of my colleagues – to just avoid leashed greetings altogether.

That's the decision we've made for Coral. We were leaning in that direction anyway, but after she and our Dalmatian were attacked by an off-leash dog several years ago that just sealed the deal. It's been a good choice for her, and in working with other dog owners, I'm more convinced it's the best choice for most if not all dogs.

Why This Is a Mistake

Allowing dogs that are meeting for the first time while both are leashed is just a recipe for problems for a number of reasons. The leash prevents the dogs from displaying normal behaviors during greetings that are designed to prevent conflict and misunderstandings.

Normal dog greetings consist of ritualized behaviors. They spend considerable time circling one another as they sniff noses and other body parts. One dog may move toward the other, and the second dog has the option of moving away. Normally initial contact occurs while both dogs have all four feet on the ground, not jumping immediately on one another.

Leashed greetings unfold entirely differently. The leash interferes with the typical circling, approach/avoidance dancing around each other.

If the dog has been pulling on the leash, by the time he gets to the other dog his front feet may be off the ground and he immediately jumps on the other dog. Most dogs don't take too kindly to that sort of inappropriate behavior. And when people keep the leashes tight and yank, jerk and pull on their dogs, this really increases the agitation and frustration and makes aggression much more likely.

The Reasons People Make This Mistake

At first glance, it's easy to think leashed greetings cause no harm, or are even enjoyable for the dogs. We know dogs are social creatures, and encountering other dogs on leash may be the only time some dogs get to see or interact with other dogs. And it's true that sometimes greetings come off without problems.

But even just one greeting that goes bad can turn your previously friendly dog into a dog-aggressive one. It's just not worth it. Ask people who have dog-aggressive dogs about what a nightmare it is to try and walk them. Maybe you're in that boat already. These problems seem to escalate quickly, and I've seen dogs that become virtually uncontrollable when they see another dog 50 yards away. These problems are much easier to prevent than they are to "fix" or resolve.

How to Create a "No Greetings" Habit

After you decide to avoid greetings with other dogs when both are leashed, the next step is to prevent greetings from taking place and then teach your dog what to do instead. How you accomplish those goals really depends on your starting place and what your dog is doing now. Here are several options:

1. Put some distance between you and the approaching dog. This may be the best and first option if your dog already is agitated and out of control at the sight of another dog. Cross the street or move to the other side of the path you are walking on. Turn a corner and take a different route. Get off the path onto a berm or other area.

2. Stop and stand in front of your dog to block your dog's sight of the other dog. If your dog won't sit still, you may need to move around a bit to keep yourself directly in front of your dog to continue to interrupt his line of sight. You can even step toward/into your dog so that he has to back up to stay out of your way. This will keep him more focused on backing up than trying to see the other dog. Keep your leash short, but as loose as possible, while you do this.

3. Refocus your dog's attention on you with treats or a toy. This will work best the quicker you do it after catching sight of the approaching dog. When this technique is implemented correctly and consistently, the sight of the other dog becomes your dog's signal that a treat or a toy is about to appear, and he will look up at you automatically.

4. Fit your dog with a Thunder Cap®, formerly known as a Calming Cap®. Although you may think your dog can't see through the Cap, he can. But the Cap filters his vision,

making objects appear fuzzy and indistinct, which in turn decreases the intensity of his response to them.

5. Pick up your pace a bit as you approach another dog. Talk to your dog with words and voice tone that encourage movement – "Come on, let's go, let's go" – making the pitch of your voice get higher.

You may need to use a no-pull harness or a head collar that we talked about in the last chapter in order to implement some of these strategies. The options are not mutually exclusive. For example, you might move to the other side of the street AND get your dog's attention with food or a toy. And you may need the help of an experienced and certified trainer, behaviorist, or behavior consultant to help you learn the motor skills required for these strategies.

Our Experience with Coral

Since we've decided not to allow on-leash greetings with Coral, she is much calmer, less excited and less agitated when she sees another dog because she knows what to expect. There is no excited anticipation, and no angst on our part wondering if this is going to go well, or not.

As Coral has gotten in the habit of not greeting other dogs, she seems less interested and just continues on her way without the whining, pulling on the leash and agitation she used to show.

And that's one of the problems with allowing on leash greetings – neither you, nor your dog, know what to expect. And that sort of uncertainty produces stress and anxiety which can lead to defensive aggression.

I don't think Coral is at all disappointed that we don't stop to say hello to other dogs. Think about all the other things about walks your dog looks forward to, as we discussed in the last chapter. The absence of close encounters with others dogs isn't really a loss when you consider the stress and uncertainty they produce.

The Exception

As I said earlier, if your dog already has doggie friends she greets on walks and does well with, there's nothing wrong with continuing those greetings. Coral has two or three dogs we greet routinely. Two are little dogs who are very calm and very friendly. The other is a very elderly Husky who just stands still while she and Coral and sniff each other.

If You Must: A Checklist

If you are determined to experiment with leash greetings, then you really need to know what to look for from both your own and the other dog's behavior as you approach.

Here's a short list:

1. The dogs' excitement level should only be "moderate". If either dog is barking, yelping, or whining uncontrollably their arousal level is likely too high for a greeting to go well.

2. Overall, both dogs should appear mostly relaxed and "wiggly". If either dog is quite tense, and looks almost driven or frantic to get to the other dog NO MATTER WHAT, the intentions are unlikely to be friendly.

3. If you hear ANY growling from either dog, do NOT allow the dogs to greet each other.

4. If the hackles are up on either dog, avoid the greeting.

5. If either dog appears to be stalking toward the other, with very deliberate steps, and in a somewhat crouched position, avoid the greeting.

6. If either dog is pulling so hard that the front feet come off the ground, the arousal level is too high and a greeting is quite risky.

Summary

My intention in this chapter was to make a good case for why on leash greetings are not worth the risk. The potential advantages of a minute or two of social contact don't outweigh the risk of creating a dog-aggressive dog as the result of one bad encounter. There is another reason why allowing leash greetings is not a good idea. Dogs get better at whatever behaviors they repeat frequently. You want to ensure your dog will "practice" behaviors you want. And that's the subject of the next chapter.

If you already have a dog-aggressive dog, seek professional help from someone who won't make any of the mistakes you'll read about in the remaining chapters. I also have a list of additional resources for you below.

Resources:

The Calming Cap®

http://www.animalbehaviorassociates.com/training-calming-cap.htm

When Cujo Meets Pavlov – a webinar course from Ms. Kathy Sdao, M.A., ACCAB on how to prevent and resolve leash aggression problems.

http://petprowebinars.com/courses-by-instructor/kathy-sdaos-classes/cujo-meets-pavlov-using-classical-conditioning-as-a-foundation-for-resolving-leash-aggression/

The links to all of the references and resources listed in this book can also be accessed from www.TerribleDogTrainingMistakes.com

Chapter 6: Practice Makes Perfect: But Not In The Way You Think

The Mistake: Allowing your dog to repeat unwanted behaviors without managing your dog's environment to prevent this.

Think of a behavior from your dog that you'd like to change. Maybe it's jumping on people at the door. Perhaps it's lunging and barking at other dogs he sees during walks. Or maybe your dog has been in the habit of lifting his leg on a chair in your formal dining room.

How many times do you think he's done each of those behaviors? A dozen? More? Let's say your dog is 2 years old and he's been jumping up on people since he was a 4 month old puppy. If someone comes to your house twice a week (that could be a really low estimate, depending on your family's lifestyle), then that equals 160 times your dog has practiced jumping up on people (20 months at 8 times/month.)

For most behaviors, that's probably a low estimate. Nancy Williams, a colleague I mentioned in the last chapter, tells me that when she has her clients make these calculations, they often come up with numbers in the thousands. Your dog is going to be quite adept at any behavior he's practiced, or repeated hundreds of times. That's the mistake -- not preventing your dog from practicing the behaviors you don't want.

The Consequences of Your Dog Practicing Unwanted Behaviors

Chances are, at some point in your life you've played a sport, taken dance or voice lessons, or played a musical instrument. Your coach or instructor without a doubt told you to practice. Why? Because of that old saying "practice makes perfect".

Practice improves performance. Or at least it should if you are practicing the right way. Our steel pan instructor is constantly reminding us that if we practice a song wrong, by playing the wrong notes, or the wrong rhythm, then we are only practicing our mistakes. It's much better to practice the song slowly, he advises us, and get the notes right so we don't have to "unlearn" our mistakes. Our instructor knows – and unfortunately I've sometimes learned the hard way because I didn't follow his advice - how much effort this "unlearning" takes and how much it delays learning to play the song the right way.

The same principle holds true with unwanted behavior from your dog. The more your dog repeats an unwanted behavior, the more difficult it becomes to change it. In addition, behaviors that are repeated are more easily triggered. They become habits that we, and our dogs, do without thinking.

Practice means your dog gets on "automatic pilot". This means the window for enticing your dog to do something else in a particular situation, may be very short, because the unwanted behavior occurs so quickly. Preventing your dog's automatic response opens up the window and makes it easier to teach another behavior. This is one definition of response prevention, which is one of the strategies to avoid the mistake of your dog repeating unwanted behaviors.

Preventing Unwanted Behaviors

There are any number of ways to prevent your dog from repeating unwanted behaviors. What strategy will be effective depends on the specific behavior and when and where it occurs. I'll discuss several of the ones I've used most often.

Environmental Management

The first is managing your dog's environment. Let's say you are housetraining your puppy or retraining your adult dog. To successfully get your dog in the habit of relieving himself outside, you must prevent him from doing so inside.

That means closing the door to the dining room, or putting up a baby gate so he can't get in there and lift his leg on the chair. As we talked about in Chapter 3, short-term confinement in a crate when a puppy can't be supervised during housetraining is an example of a response prevention technique.

If your dog is barking and fence running with the neighbor dog you can't expect to successfully modify that behavior if you leave him outside and let him do that uninterrupted for hours on end while you are at work. You'll need to bring him inside, or create some kind of inner barrier outside to prevent your dog from getting to the fence.

The Use of Restraint to Prevent a Response

Another strategy is to use a safe and humane way of restraint. A leash and any harness, collar, or halter (head collar) is an example of restraint. Ashley and Coral both have on Gentle Leaders® in the following picture .

When it comes to jumping up on visitors, you can easily prevent the behavior by simply putting a leash and collar on your dog before you answer the door. Stand on the leash, or tie it to a nearby object. Adjust the length of the leash so while your dog has all four feet on the ground, and is standing in one place, he feels no tension whatsoever. If he attempts to jump, the leash will be short enough to prevent jumping.   During the seconds he's not trying to jump, reward him with petting and treats.

A harness or head collar, properly used, prevents pulling on leash, as I discussed in Chapter 4. You can use certain types of head collars – especially the <u>Snoot Loop</u>, to close your dog's mouth and prevent him from barking. But that's not the only way restraint can be used to prevent an unwanted response.

Don't get the wrong impression about restraint. I'm talking about techniques I'm guessing you've never heard of. I'm certainly not referring to leash and collar "corrections" or anything meant to be aversive.

Case Example

Not too long ago I worked with a little dog who became quite agitated at the sight of other dogs. Even if the other dog was 20 feet away, she'd rear up on her hind legs, pull on the leash, and begin barking and growling. She was oblivious to any attempts her owner made to distract her. The behavior had gotten so bad her owner had stopped taking her for walks. I decided to employ a response prevention technique.

We made a visit to the local dog park, but stayed outside in the parking lot. Rather than allowing little Princess to become agitated as she watched the dogs come and go, I wrapped her tightly in a towel and held her. This prevented the on-leash behaviors that had become "automatic" and were contributing to her arousal in a detrimental feedback loop.

While snugly wrapped in the towel, Princess could see other dogs but was prevented from lunging and pulling on her leash. She learned she didn't have to do those behaviors after all. Other dogs could walk by and nothing bad was going to happen even if she didn't go through her agitated routine. She began to learn a new habit – calmly watching dogs as they passed by.

Tweaking Response Prevention. Sometimes a dog's response is so intense that preventing it is quite difficult, and could even be dangerous for either you or your dog. Princess was a tiny little dog and easy to hold, but the same wouldn't be true for a 90 pound Rottweiler. That's when it's best to start gradually, with a situation that won't cause your dog to be completely wound up.

In Princess's case, we stood back a few feet from where the dogs were entering the park, to keep some distance between us. I also left a flap of towel free so that if Princess started to wiggle in the towel because she was getting too aroused, I could flip the towel over her eyes to block her sight of the dogs. The Calming Cap™ we've talked about in other chapters can be used in the same way.

In less than an hour, Princess was watching dogs go by without barking or trying to wiggle out of the towel. I had begun giving her a tiny piece of corned beef (her favorite treat) each time a new dog passed by. Her owner reported that was the calmest Princess had been in the presence of another dog in years.

Quite a few steps would still be needed to get to the point of Princess being able to pass other dogs on a leash relatively calmly, but at least we finally had a behavioral starting point.

My Best Advice

Some trainers may try and tell you that response prevention doesn't fit with training based on positive reinforcement. This reflects confusion about what response prevention is. Many trainers use harnesses and head collars to prevent behaviors, so they are using response prevention already whether they realize it or not.

It would be ludicrous for any trainer to claim that managing a dog's environment to prevent unwanted behavior is inappropriate (assuming your method of doing so isn't harming the dog, as with excessive crating). If someone is telling you that, you might want to find another trainer.

Second, some trainers confuse response prevention with punishment. Consider the towel example with Princess. I didn't wrap Princess in the towel *after* she was barking and lunging. I did it before we stepped out of the car at the dog park. Punishment starts after a behavior, not before it.

Third, there's no reason to think Princess found being held in a towel aversive. That's what punishment is – applying something aversive following a behavior. There is another kind of punishment, but we'll talk about that in Chapter 10.

When you stop to think about it, becoming agitated, aroused, and even frightened when Princess saw other dogs was much more unpleasant than being held safely in a towel, quietly watching other dogs pass by her.

Summary

Has your dog practiced one or more unwanted behaviors so that now he is an expert at displaying them quickly? To further convince yourself of how practice has made those behaviors perfect, tally up how many times your dog has repeated a behavior you want to change.

How can you use either environmental management or safe restraint to interrupt the behavior and prevent additional practice? We talked about harnesses, head collars, leashes, baby gates, and more. Preventing the unwanted behavior may be the puzzle piece you've been missing if you've been unsuccessful getting your dog to what you want. But a word of caution. Preventing the behavior doesn't mean grabbing your dog's collar, or jerking him around on a leash. That's actually terrible training mistake number seven which we'll cover in the next chapter "I Wouldn't Do That If I Were You".

Now that we've gotten deep into the 12 terrible training mistakes, I hope you are starting to see how interrelated many of the mistakes are.

Resources Mentioned in This Chapter

The Calming Cap™
http://www.animalbehaviorassociates.com/training-calming-cap.htm

The Snoot Loop®
http://www.snootloop.com

The Gentle Leader®
http://www.petsafe.net/gentleleader

The links to all of the references and resources listed in this book can also be accessed from www.TerribleDogTrainingMistakes.com

Chapter 7: I Wouldn't Do That If I Were You

The Mistake: Using confrontational and physical procedures to train your dog.

Early in my dog training career, I trained a Dalmatian named Peaches. Peaches was an absolutely gorgeous dog and the sweetest, friendliest dog toward people you could ask for. She did not always do well with other dogs. My training mentor at the time advised me that if Peaches threatened or tried to bite another dog, I should grab her and pin her to the ground so she would know this was unacceptable behavior. This so-called "alpha roll", and the related "scruff shake", were standard techniques for disciplining dogs in the early 1980s. They'd been made popular in the book "How to Be Your Dog's Best Friend" by the Monks of New Skete, and one Job Michael Evans.

I'm ashamed to admit, years later, that I did roll and pin Peaches a number of times back then for her threats to other dogs. One night after a training class, while chatting with friends, Peaches again went after another dog. Before I could move a muscle, Peaches then threw herself on the floor in the exact same position I'd previously pinned her in.

At that point I realized despite my months of disciplinary efforts, all Peaches had learned was to throw herself on the ground after threatening another dog. Pinning her had taught her NOTHING about how to get along with other dogs. That was a light bulb minute for me. I knew that this punishment-based approach was severely flawed, and I had much to learn about how best to teach Peaches to behave around other dogs.

Why Confrontational and Physical Methods Are a Mistake

Have you ever heard the phrase violence begets violence? While it may be a biblical reference, it's also a quote from Martin Luther King from 1958. According to a recent study 57% of mothers and 40% of fathers spank their 3-year-olds. Yet the research links spanking to several negative effects on behavioral development and language acquisition[1]. Experts say spanking teaches children that the way to get others to do what you want is to hit them.

You may be arguing that you were spanked, or you spanked your kids and you turned out OK and so did they. Well, I "alpha rolled" my dogs a few times in the 1980s, and they did "OK" but:

1. How much better could they have done if I hadn't done that?

2. In Peaches case, it certainly didn't help her behavior, and likely contributed to her continuing problems with other dogs.

3. I was probably damn lucky that being confrontational with the dogs didn't cause more problems or cause me to be bitten. This was likely because they were all friendly dogs with stable temperaments in the first place. What would have happened if Peaches or any of my own dogs had tendencies to be aggressive to people? Chances are, I would have been bitten.

4. Why would I, or anyone, insist on using confrontational or corporal techniques if I knew they really didn't accomplish my goals, and if there were effective ways to address problems that didn't require them?

One answer to the last question is that confrontational techniques continue to be used because they do result in short-term behavioral suppression in at least some dogs. That gives the illusion that "they work". Another reason is because they allow the people delivering them to release their own frustration anger.

"Alpha rolls" and "scruff shakes" claimed the Monks and Job Evans, mimicked how dogs "discipline" each other. Like the "alpha wolf" myth, that statement is an untruth. Here's why.

What Behavioral Science Has to Say

When one dog submits to another, there is either no physical contact, or it's very restrained and inhibited. Take a look at the picture below.

The little dog is choosing to roll over on her back. Neither of the big dogs have her by the throat. If you grab your dog by the collar, the neck, or the shoulders, and throw her to the ground, it's more like one of these big dogs grabbing the little one by the throat and shaking her. That's a life-threatening fight, not a ritualized display communicating "I'm not happy with your behavior".

What can dogs be expected to do when they fear for their safety? They fight back. Research from veterinary behaviorist Dr. Meghan Herron and her colleagues, revealed that when confrontational techniques are used with dogs (in the study these included hitting, kicking, growling at the dog, prying objects out of mouth, "dominance down", staring, grab dog by jowls and shake, and more), they caused an aggressive response in about a quarter of the dogs they were used on[2]. Dogs that had a history of aggression toward familiar people were more likely to respond with aggression to "alpha rolls" and being yelled at, than dogs with other types of behavior problems.

The dogs that respond with aggression often get labeled as "dominant" when in reality they are defensive, with social status being completely irrelevant.

If a dog chooses not to fight back, you may instead see extreme signs of fear, a topic we will take up in Chapter 9.

"Alpha rolls" and "scruff shakes" should be completely OFF the table as far as choices of how to try to train or punish your dog. Before his death, **Job Michael Evans apologized for ever suggesting these techniques.** You'll find a link to the story about the apology at the end of this chapter.

Grabbing Your Dog's Collar

Alpha rolls and scruff shakes aren't the only confrontational or physical techniques to be avoided. Grabbing your dog's collar is another one. I've seen many cases of aggression caused by this habit. Your dog can quickly learn that when you grab his collar, bad things happen. If you drag him over to show him his "mess" (you'll learn in Chapter 8 why trying to show your dog the results of his misbehavior is a terrible mistake) even one time, the next time you grab for his collar he may snap at you.

The only time to grab for a collar is in an emergency situation, when you need to prevent your dog from getting in harm's way, and you don't trust having verbal control.

Your Homework

Try this experiment for a couple of days. If your dog wears a collar regularly, take it off when you are home. If your dog is secure in your home or yard, there's no risk. (In fact, if you leave your dog home alone with a collar on you are risking a strangulation death). You'll discover within just a few hours how much you are relying on collar grabs to control your dog.

Alternatives

Not having the option of grabbing your dog's collar to control him helps you more quickly learn ways to get your dog to do what you want so you can reward her. I've not had my dogs wear collars around the house for 30 years. If I need one of my dogs to come to me, and away from something else, I call her. I can also move in front of her and/or step into her and block her forward motion or have her move backwards.

My good friend and colleague Ms. Kathy Sdao, M.A., ACAAB told me a great story about the time she dropped an entire prime rib roast on her kitchen floor. Her dogs were hanging about in the kitchen as usual, and when the roast landed they both immediately started toward it, thinking of course that Kathy had dropped it there for them. What would you have done? Yelled NO NO!? Grabbed their collars? That's a set-up for a bite, especially if one of your children did it, trying to help.

What did Kathy do? Told her dogs to sit. Which they did, and were rewarded with some prime rib.

Prying Your Dog's Mouth Open

As you've surmised, our Irish setter Coral is definitely a "bird dog". She comes from championship field lines and her absolute primary goal in life is to hunt for birds. Coral views all walks as just that – bird hunts. Recently, during a leash walk, Coral was quick enough to grab a Gambel's Quail that got itself caught on a tall cactus trying to fly away from her. Being the great field dog she is (although we've never hunted with her), Coral very gently held the bird in her mouth. I knew from her behavior that she thought this was the BEST thing that had ever happened to her *(MOM – I finally got a BIRD, I GOT A BIRD!)*. I resisted my very first instinct which was to rush toward her and try to open her mouth with my hands. I knew if I did this, she would clamp down and the bird would be a goner. Although I knew Coral wouldn't purposely bite me, I wasn't too sure I could keep my fingers out of the way if she made a second grab for the bird.

Instead, in a very calm voice, I said what I usually say when I want her to stop sniffing or stop staring at a bunny and move along on our walk. "Come on Coral, let's go, let's go for our walk, come on". After several repetitions she dropped the bird, which toddled off into the bushes, appearing literally weak from fright. I did not scream "LEAVE IT" OR "PUT IT DOWN", which would have had no effect other than to frighten Coral, convince her something was wrong, and decrease the chances she'd let go of the bird.

Prying the bird out of her mouth would have been the exact wrong thing to do for all those reasons. Several of my colleagues are convinced that prying a dog's mouth open is a contributing factor to the problem of pica – eating of non-food objects. These are the dogs that ingest socks, rocks and other objects that can create life-threatening intestinal blockages. At the least, when a dog expects to have her mouth pried open and a coveted object removed, she's more likely to swallow it before this can happen. That means your dog is more likely to swallow potentially dangerous items she's "stolen" from the trash or someplace else when she sees you coming toward her.

Repeated use of this technique can also make it more difficult to open your dog's mouth to give her a pill. Past episodes of mouth prying have been associated with anger and angst.

What To Do Instead. If you MUST get something away from your dog, trade him for something better. In fact, this is the first step in a training protocol to teach your dog to drop something when asked. If you can move him away from the object after he drops it even better. Get in the habit of calling your dog into the kitchen for a "cookie"/biscuit out of the treat jar. That allows someone else to go retrieve the forbidden item without a confrontation.

Summary

In this chapter we covered only three of the most problematic techniques that can cause dogs to respond aggressively or react in other unwanted ways. These are alpha rolls or scruff shakes, grabbing your dog's collar, and prying something out of her mouth. I'm assuming that kicking, hitting, or slapping your dog are completely off the table as options from the get-go.

I've tried to avoid the rhetoric and tell you, based on what we know scientifically about dog behavior and learning, and from my own experience, why these techniques are mistakes.

When research and experience so clearly show these and other confrontational or physical techniques are so risky, and so many better options exist, there's no reason to use or rely on them.

The same holds true when we have research to show dogs do not know right from wrong, or experience guilt. That's the subject of our next chapter "But He Knows Better!"

Resources Mentioned in This Chapter

The apology from Job Michael Evans story

http://beyondcesarmillan.weebly.com/ehowcom.html

References

[1] MacKenzie, M.J., Nicklas, E., Waldfogel, J., and J. Brooks-Gunn, 2013. Spanking and Child Development Across the First Decade of Life. Pediatrics,. Available online –

http://pediatrics.aappublications.org/content/early/2013/10/16/peds.2013-1227.full.pdf+html

[2] Herron, M. E. et al., 2009. Survey of the use and outcome of confrontational and non-confrontational training methods in client-owned dogs showing undesired behaviors. Journal of Applied Animal Behaviour Science 117(1):47-54.
Read the abstract using the link below.
http://www.appliedanimalbehaviour.com/article/S0168-1591%2808%2900371-7/abstract

The links to all of the references and resources listed in this book can also be accessed from www.TerribleDogTrainingMistakes.com

Chapter 8: But He Knows Better

The Mistake: Believing your dog knows right from wrong and other anthropomorphic interpretations of dog behavior

You come home and you know right away your dog has gotten into trouble while you've been gone. Why? Because he isn't greeting you at the door. Instead, he's nowhere to be found. Or if he does greet you, you know from how he looks that he's guilty about something. He may slink toward you, rather than bounding up to you with his usual happy demeanor. .

Sure enough, when you look around you find the evidence of your dog's misbehavior. Trash strewn across the house, pee or poop on the floor, couch cushions shredded, or any number of possible items destroyed or damaged.

Your dog looks guilty – his ears are back, his tail is tucked, he's ducking his head and/or he's avoiding you. If he's really upset, he might even roll over and urinate on himself. All of these behaviors mean he knows what he did was wrong – by your standards – and he's guilty about and sorry for his behavior. Right? **WRONG!!!**

Why This Is a Mistake

To cut right to the chase, dogs do not have a moral sense of right and wrong. There is no evidence that other non-human animals do either (and clearly evidence that some humans don't as well! But that's the subject for a different book!)

Dogs Are Good At Learning What Happens Next

What dogs ARE very good at doing is making discriminations about when their behavior is likely to cause something unpleasant to happen and when it won't. For example, if you scold your dog every time you see him get in the trash he'll learn it's a good idea to avoid the trash when you are there to scold him. The more consistent you are about scolding him every time he sticks his nose in the trash, the sooner he'll stop doing it. Of course the other rule is that your scolding has to be more UNPLEASANT than the pleasant experience of finding goodies in the trash.

Let's say that after a couple of scoldings, your dog rarely if ever, puts his nose in the trash when you're there. You could conclude that he's learned getting into the trash is "wrong". But you'd be wrong instead!

What your dog has learned is that something unpleasant happens when you see him stick his nose in the trash. As a result, he's decided not to let you see him get into the trash. What do you think happens when he sticks his nose in the trash when you aren't there to see him do it?

OH HAPPY DAY!! Your dog pulls out that chicken skin from last night's dinner, or the wrap from the ice cream sandwich that still has a bit of chocolate attached to it and chows down. **OH HAPPY DAY!!** Your dog has been rewarded, big time, for sticking his nose in the trash. So how can he possibly think sticking his nose in the trash is wrong? Because from his perspective it isn't.

For your dog, there is no "right" or "wrong" to these situations, only behavioral consequences. Sticking his nose in the trash in your presence results in unpleasant consequences. Doing the same thing when you aren't around is quite enjoyable and rewarding.

Submission Not Guilt

The second part of this mistake is labeling the behaviors you see from your dog as "guilty looks". They are not. They are submissive behaviors. The purpose of submissive behaviors is to terminate threats. When you see "the mess", your behavior instantly changes and your dog knows bad things are looming. To "turn off" or prevent your threatening behavior, your dog turns on all his species-typical behaviors that for thousands of years have evolved to keep him safe against threatening opponents. His ears go back and his tail goes down. His eyes may get squinty, and he lowers his head and ducks into a crouch. He may grin (show his teeth) submissively and even urinate. The message is "stop threatening me, I give in". The message is NOT "I know I shouldn't have done it"

It's Easy To Be Confused

That discrepancy of not trash-diving in your presence, but continuing to do so when you aren't there, is one reason why dog owners conclude their dogs "know better". And there is a grain of truth in that. Your dog knows better than to trash-dive in your presence. But that's MUCH different from concluding your dog knows that trash-diving overall is "wrong". He very much knows that trash-diving when he's alone is a wonderful thing.

The second reason for believing your dog "knows better", is how your dog behaves when you come home and find a "mess". The "mess" could be anything whose presence has caused you to get upset and angry. Most often the "mess" is some evidence of destructive behavior, or the presence of urine or feces.

Your dog has learned that in the presence of a "mess" AND you, bad things will happen. You don't necessarily have to see the mess for your dog to have connected the dots between a "mess" somewhere in the house, your presence, and subsequent punishment.

If you are there and there is no mess (minus mess), good things happen as you greet your dog. If the mess is there and you aren't (minus you), nothing bad happens so your dog behaves normally.

Do you really think your dog walks around the house looking or feeling "guilty" all day after getting into the trash? Of course not! And that is the key point. The behaviors that dog owners attribute to "guilt" are in fact triggered by the owners' very presence, NOT by the production of "the mess". In fact, there are several recent and very creative studies that prove just that.

Dogs are Socially Sensitive

Dr. Alexandra Horowitz[1] set up a very creative set of four circumstances that teased apart the dogs' behavior from the owners' reactions. In all circumstances, the dog was left alone with a piece of food that the owner had told the dog not to eat before leaving the room. Can you guess what the four circumstances were?

1. The dog was fed the piece of food by the experimenter (in the owner's absence) but upon her return, the owner was told the dog did NOT eat it and to greet the dog normally.

2. The dog was fed the piece of food by the experimenter and upon her return, the owner was told the dog DID eat it and to scold the dog.

3. The dog did not eat the food but the owner was told he did and asked to scold her dog.

4. The dog did not eat the food, and the owner was told that he did not eat it, and asked to greet the dog normally.

Hopefully, you can predict the results. The dogs that "looked guilty" were the dogs that were scolded, whether or not they ate the food. Interestingly, the dogs were more submissive ("guilty") when scolded when they had NOT eaten the food.

The term "socially sensitive" has been applied to dogs' reactions, meaning that dogs are tremendously attuned to our behaviors. There is additional evidence that socially sensitive behaviors benefit dogs. In a follow-up study, behaviorist Julie Hecht[2] and her team found that owners are less likely to scold their dogs when the dogs show the submissive behaviors. See – submissive behaviors work as designed!

When There is No "Evidence"

Another way to convince yourself that "punishment after the fact" isn't effective is to consider how you would respond if your neighbor told you your dog had been barking all day. Would you immediately rush up to your dog and yell at him? I hope not. Without any "evidence" of misbehavior you would know your dog wouldn't have a clue as to why you were screaming at him. Your dog has the same reaction whether there is "evidence" or not. He does not connect "evidence" with behavior.

Taking the Blame

If you have multiple dogs, you might have observed something similar to the following. If one dog shows submissive behaviors when you come home and find a mess and the other one does not, you'd likely assume the submissive dog did the deed. And according to Hecht's research, you just might be wrong. In her study, owners were not very accurate at predicting whether or not their dog had eaten the forbidden treat. So even though one dog acts submissively, he may NOT be the one who misbehaved.

You Can Avoid This Mistake

No good will come of attempting to punish your dog for behaviors you didn't see, regardless of whether there is "evidence" of the misbehavior. When there is a time delay between a behavior and the punishment, the consequence is not contingent (dependent) on the behavior. This means the punishment isn't connected to the behavior. Punishment that comes out of the blue, isn't predictable, and therefore isn't avoidable, has long been known to cause animals (and people as well) a great deal of stress and anxiety.

After-the-fact punishment not only won't stop the behavior you want to stop, it will also create a dog that is reluctant to do what you want in other situations because he doesn't trust you, and may be quite fearful of you because in his eyes you are quite unpredictable.

And by the way, punishment (and reinforcement as well) is defined by its effect on behavior. Punishment decreases the likelihood or frequency of a behavior. If that doesn't happen, then by definition, whatever you've done is not punishment. Instead, it's just bad treatment of your dog.

What To Do Instead

So what's the right response when you come home and find a "mess"? Take a deep breath, get hold of your temper and greet your dog normally. Or if you can't quite manage that, at least ignore him in a neutral way. Don't stomp around the house muttering under your breath. There is nothing you can do right then to your dog that will effectively prevent the behavior from happening again. But there is A LOT you can do that will harm your dog and your relationship with him. So make the right choice.

More importantly, you'll need to figure out why he's doing the annoying behavior in your absence, and find a way to change his behavior. If the problem is essentially foraging behavior, (getting into the trash, jumping on the kitchen counters) the answer is to either not give your dog access to the goodies, or make trying to get to the goodies immediately unpleasant with the use of harmless "booby traps".

You could for example, simply put the trash in the garage or in a cabinet under the sink rather than leaving it as fair game for your dog. Perhaps you install child-proof locks on your cabinets so your dog can't paw them open and get into the snacks.

Or you could surround your trash with a Scat Mat™ . The Scat Mat™ is a vinyl mat with wires embedded so that it delivers a mild static shock (like touching a metal object after you've walked across carpet in a dry climate) when touched. The sensation is unpleasant, and causes most dogs to get off the mat quite quickly, and to avoid it in the future. Other "booby traps" include motion detectors that emit a loud noise, either audible or ultrasonic, and/or a harmless spray, when activated by your dog's presence (A Scraminal® is one option; the Stay Away® combines sound and compressed air and the SSSCAT® is a spray only, a good option for dogs that are overly sound sensitive.)

There are many other reasons for home-alone misbehaviors such as housesoiling or destructiveness. You'll have to decipher the motivation first before deciding what to do. If your dog is afraid of being left alone, that would require a very different behavior modification plan than if your dog was frightened from a noise phobia, if he was marking territory in response to dogs outside, or if he was tearing up the couch cushions for lack of anything better to do. You may require help from a certified behaviorist, trainer, or behavior consultant to help you determine the motivation for your dog's home-alone behaviors and how best to change them. You can also consult the resource list for these problems at the end of this chapter.

Summary

I am so grateful for the work of creative behavior researchers who finally have objective data for what so many of us who work with dogs have been telling people for so long. It may make you feel better to lose your temper at your dog when you find a mess, but it harms your dog much more than it benefits you. That's why it's one of the 12 terrible training mistakes.

In this chapter you've learned why it's true that your dog doesn't really "know better", and what you can do to investigate, prevent, and modify behaviors that occur in your absence.

In the next chapter we'll continue talking about miscommunications. Because it turns out that interpreting submissive behaviors as "guilty looks" is just the tip of the iceberg.

Resources Mentioned in this Chapter

The Scat Mat®
http://store.petsafe.net/scatmat-curved-mat

The Scraminal®

http://www.amazon.com/Amtek-Scraminal/dp/B002D8PKOS

The SSSCat

http://www.contech-inc.com/products/home-and-garden-products/animal-repellents/stayaway-motion-activated-pet-deterrent

The Stay Away ®

http://www.contech-inc.com/products/home-and-garden-products/animal-repellents/stayaway-motion-activated-pet-deterrent,)

Additional Resources

Three session webinar course **"Help For Home Alone Dogs".** Available at PetProWebinars.com

http://petprowebinars.com/courses-by-instructor/help-for-home-alone-dogs/. Designed primarily for the pet professional.

"Helping the Home Alone Fido" – a DVD program that includes handouts and specific protocols for your to implement. Designed for the dog owner.

http://animalbehaviorassociates.com/dvd-helpingthehomealonefido.htm

"I'll Be Home Soon" – a book by our good friend and colleague Patricia McConnell, Ph.D., CAAB that helps dog owners understand, prevent, and manage separation anxiety problems http://www.patriciamcconnell.com/store/I-ll-Be-Home-Soon.html

References

[1] Horowitz, A. 2009. Disambiguating the "guilty look": salient prompts to a familiar dog behavior. Behavioural Processes 81 (3): 447-452.

[2] Hecht, J., Miklosi, A. and Gacsi, M., 2012. Behavioral assessment and owner perceptions of behaviors associated with guilt in dogs. Applied Animal Behaviour Science 139 (1-2): 134-142.

The links to all of the references and resources listed in this book can also be accessed from www.TerribleDogTrainingMistakes.com

Chapter 9: What We Have is a Failure to Communicate

The Mistake: Not recognizing signs of fear and anxiety from your dog.

Years ago, we owned a self-service dog wash from a franchise called Laund-ur-Mutt®. As one of our regular customers was drying his dog with the dryer, the dog was sitting on the grooming table, leaning against the wall, yawning repeatedly. Our customer said that was how he could tell his dog really liked his baths, because he was so relaxed during them he would yawn and almost fall asleep.

Oh my. His dog was anything but relaxed. The reason the dog was leaning against the wall was because he was trying to get as far away from the dryer as possible. He'd pulled his ears back against his head, and his tail was tucked tight in a half circle against his legs. Both of these are body postures typical of fearful dogs.

Yawning in this context was not a sign of relaxation. Instead, it's what behaviorists call a *displacement behavior*. These are normal behaviors that are *displaced* out of their usual context. They are an indication the dog is uncertain and somewhat anxious about what to do. The dog is conflicted about doing one behavior versus another, so to resolve the conflict he does neither. Instead, he chooses a displacement behavior.

In Fido's case, the dog's choices were to jump down off the table (risking the displeasure of and a "correction" from his owner) or stay where he was. As he was trying to decide which was the lesser of two evils for him, he yawned to manage his conflict and anxiety.

Granted, that description is a bit anthropomorphic, but nevertheless the existence of displacement behaviors in conflict situations is well established. And like our customer, most dog owners either do not notice them, misinterpret their meaning, or aren't aware such behaviors are extremely important in understanding their dog's behavior.

Recent research bears out our experiences with dog owners. Dr. Michele Wan, a Certified Applied Animal Behaviorist, and our friend and colleague, found that dog owners and professionals with less than 10 years of experience had more trouble identifying signs of fear, stress and anxiety from dogs than did professionals with over 10 years of experience.

Dr. Wan's research* further tells us that regardless of our experience with dogs, people are mostly able to identify when a dog is happy. It's identifying the fear, stress, and anxiety that trips people up. Because most bites occur from fearful dogs, missing these signs can have very bad consequences. At the very least, allowing stress, anxiety, and fear to go unrecognized in our dogs prevents us from either relieving or preventing these conditions, decreases their quality of life, and can even contribute to disease and a variety of behavior problems.

The Reasons People Make This Mistake

Displacement behaviors are a specialized group of behaviors that you'd be unlikely to know about unless you'd talked to a behavior professional or taken an animal behavior course. Much of the information about canine communication signals that is more easily accessible to the general public in the popular media is either incomplete or just plain wrong.

For example most people have been taught that a wagging tail that indicates a dog is friendly. While a tail that is furiously wagging in a wide sweeping motion is probably a sign of friendliness, a more measured stiff-looking side-to-side wag is part of an offensive threat. But the popular media usually doesn't tell you that.

Second, there's a real difference between casually watching your dog versus carefully observing his body postures and how they change from moment to moment.

And there's also a difference between observing behaviors and interpreting them. You likely have a lot of experience watching your dog's behaviors. Nobody spends more time with your dog than you do. You are best able to notice when her behavior changes because you know what's normal, and typical for her. But you may not always know what features of your dog's body language are more important, or how to interpret what you see. Remember our Laund-ur-Mutt® customer and his yawning dog.

I'll spend the rest of this chapter improving your observational skills and tell you the different features of your dog's body to pay attention to, so you will better know when your dog is scared, anxious or stressed.

How Your Dog Communicates

Your dog reveals his intentions and emotions through his body language. To know whether your dog is fearful and stressed (or in some other emotional state), you shouldn't depend on just one feature. Your dog's ears may be telling you one thing, while her tail tells you something else. It's not uncommon for your dog to be ambivalent, confused, or "of two minds" about how's she's feeling in a particular moment. The more careful attention you pay to your dog – the more features of her body you look at – the more information you'll have about your dog's emotional state.

I'm going to tell you how to observe and interpret six features of your dog's body that will give you clues as to whether she's fearful, stressed or anxious.

Those are the important emotional states this chapter is about helping you recognize. I'm focusing on those because when they are missed, it impacts your dog's quality of life, makes bites more likely, and because the research shows people in general are not good at recognizing them. Recognizing these states ties into a number of the other terrible dog training mistakes in this book, namely Chapters 5, 8, 10 and 12.

1. Your Dog's Overall Body Carriage When your dog is fearful she won't stand up tall and straight. Instead, you'll notice her lower her head, crouch down a little or a lot, or even roll over if she is quite fearful (although rolling over is more associated with submission rather than fear). Look at our Dalmatian Mocha in the following top picture. He's reacting to Dan reaching over his head. Compare that to Mocha's more upright posture in the following bottom picture where Dan is demonstrating the correct way to greet a dog.

Watch what your dog does with her body in reaction to your interaction with her. Does what you are doing cause her to duck her head or crouch down? That means what you are doing is frightening or intimidating her (she could be showing submission – there's a fair amount of overlap between the two, but some differences as well). Is that your intention?

What if she responds this way when a child reaches out to pet her? If the child not only tries to pet, but to hug her as well, your dog could become sufficiently frightened to bite, because she finds it necessary to protect herself. That's why it's so important to pay attention to these initial, subtle signs.

2. Your Dog's Body Position Relative to You or Others

A fearful dog wants to fly under the radar, so to speak. She doesn't want to create conflict or inadvertently challenge her social partner. To avoid being a challenge, she'll turn her body a bit so that she's not approaching another individual straight on. It may appear as though your dog has turned the side of her body to you, as she sort of angles into you sideways. Look at how Coral has turned, and is refusing to face Ashley during a conflict over the toys.

What if your dog is running confidently toward you to say hello, or perhaps after you've called her. As she comes, you notice her paws are muddy and you don't want to get dirty. So you yell at her "Fido NO!!". Your dog slows down and now angles toward you in a big half circle. You may have accomplished your goal of not getting muddy, but you've also frightened your dog when she was doing a very good thing – happily running toward you. Was that your intention?

3. Your Dog's Tail position

Not all dogs have tails! When dogs have very short or docked tails we, and they, have lost a communication feature. When your dog is fearful, she will carry her tail lower than normal. Compare Coral's tail carriage in the following two pictures.

Obviously, it's important to know what's normal for your dog. Start to notice her tail carriage when she's just walking around, calm and relaxed so you'll easily be able to tell when her tail is lower than normal. If she's really frightened, there won't be a question – it could be tucked between her legs during extreme fear.

If your dog is only slightly fearful, she might wag her tail a little from side to side. But you won't see the high, full tail wag from a confident, happy dog.

Your dog can shift her tail (and ear) carriage very quickly. In the muddy dog example, chances are your dog lowered her tail at the same time she changed the angle of her approach to you. Watch your dog's tail position the next time you talk to her, or even look at her. Your dog might lower her tail just when you stare at her. That's because staring is intimidating. Was that your intention?

4. Your Dog's Ear carriage

Dr. Wan found that the less experience people had being around dogs, the more they relied on the dog's tail to give them information. More experienced people paid attention to the ears. So ear position is an under-utilized piece of information!

That may be because floppy or dropped ears are hard to see as are those that are the same color as the rest of the dog's coat, without any highlights or markings.

If your dog has upright or "pricked" ears, when she's fearful she'll lower or flatten them. She may flatten them out to the side, or against the back of her head. This is what the dog in the following picture is doing, because the child's behavior is frightening her.

Some dogs have the ability to flatten one ear and not the other. Dogs with cropped ears cannot flatten them. Cropped ears and docked tails reduce a dog's ability to communicate effectively and normally. Not a good thing.

If your dog has floppy ears, she'll pull them backwards when she's frightened or intimidated. Take a look at our Brandy's ears in the picture below.

This contrasts with what your dog does with her ears when you ask her if she wants to go for a walk or a car ride. She'll likely pull them forward. This is what Brandy is doing in the picture below. Contrast her ear position with the previous picture.

Notice where your dog's ears are right before you tell her to sit or to lie down. Then ask her to do one of those behaviors, or any other word that she knows, such as shake hands or roll over. Did her ear carriage change when you asked her to do something? What about her tail?

If you answered yes, she's likely a bit intimidated or frightened by your request. Had you thought about that before? I want my dog Coral to be happy when I ask her to sit or come to me, in anticipation of something good. If your dog's ears or tail drop significantly when you tell her to sit, you might have followed the "because I said so" method of training I'll talk about in the next chapter. Try some retraining using the reward based approach I'll talk about in Chapter 11.

5. Your Dog's Eyes and Where She's Looking

When your dog is afraid or anxious, she won't look directly at whatever it is that is making her feel that way. If it's a noise, there may not be one place to look because she can't identify where thunder, for example, is coming from. In that case you might see your dog look rapidly around in all directions. But if she is afraid of a person, or another animal, your dog is unlikely to look right at the individual. Stares and eye contact are confrontational, and that's the last thing a fearful dog wants. Instead, she'll look away and turn her head to the side, or toward the ground, often as part of lowering her head and neck. She may look at you for a second, but look away again.

Avoiding eye contact is a big component of what gets labeled as "guilty looks" that we talked about in Chapter 8. Looking away isn't a sign of guilt, but of fear, anxiety or submission. It means your dog is responding to something she finds threatening or intimidating. In the following picture, the dog is looking away from the baby he is afraid of. Also notice the dog's ears are pulled back, and his eyes have that wide open, fearful appearance I describe next.

Many trainers recommend teaching dogs to maintain eye contact (have you heard of "Watch Me"?), so they know the dog is paying attention to them. Having a dog pay attention is a good thing, but I think we need to recognize what eye contact communicates in the dog's way of looking at things.

Next time your dog looks away from you or avoids making eye contact, analyze what you are doing. Why is your – or someone else's - behavior causing your dog to be fearful and look away?

When your dog is fearful you may be able to notice that she has a wide eyed look and her pupils are dilated. Because her eyes are so wide open, you'll also see more of the whites of her eyes that surround the pupil and the colored iris. This is different from a somewhat "squinty" (tension around the eyes, giving eyes a smaller, more slit-like than open, round appearance), hard look some dogs assume when they are aggressively motivated and the muscles in their faces are very tense.

Let's say your dog is lying on the floor, and your toddler starts to crawl toward her. Your dog turns her head to the side, and her eyes get really big. Now you know your dog is letting you know that the baby crawling toward her scares her. If she can't get out of the way fast enough, this sets up a situation for your dog to snap at your child. So when you see the head turn and the big eyes, it's time for you to take action by either calling your dog or picking up your child.

6. Your Dog's Face and Mouth

Fearful or anxious dogs often pant. Take a look at the picture of the fearful dog below.

They may also whine, yelp or even bark. Fearful barking tends to be pitched higher than the deep sounding barks of a threatening or aggressive dog.

Dogs that are *only* fearful, and not threatening or aggressive, will not show their teeth. There is one exception. Some dogs, when they are quite intimidated, or even as part of a friendly greeting, will submissively grin. They raise their lips to show their teeth in the front of their mouths. If you've not seen a submissive grin before you may at first think the dog is threatening you, but she is not.

Displacement Behaviors

At the beginning of this chapter, I explained what displacement behaviors are and under what conditions dog show them. Yawning is a very common displacement behavior in dogs which is what you see the dog in the picture below doing because he is anxious about the child trying to pet him.

A second displacement behavior is lip licking. You might have seen your dog touch the tip of his tongue to his nose, or run his tongue around his lips. While dogs normally lick their lips in anticipation of food, displacement lip licking occurs when your dog is unsure about what to do next.

Coral often lip licks or yawns when we put her harness on to go for a walk. She dislikes wearing her harness (or any collar) but she really loves walks. She's conflicted about standing still to have her harness put on, so she yawns or licks her lips. Look at our Dalmatian Ashley doing a lip-lick in the picture below. She was uncertain about how to react when we pointed our camera at her.

A third displacement activity you've probably seen from your dog is self-grooming, usually in the form of scratching.

It's normal for a dog to lick her coat, and scratch herself. But when these grooming activities occur at high frequencies or in unexpected situations, they are displacement behaviors. We see many dogs scratch excessively while at the veterinary clinic, during training class, and sometimes when dogs are in a room with lots of visitors at home.

The Value of Displacement Behaviors

Because displacement activities indicate your dog is uncertain about what to do next, think of them as your early warning signs that your dog is stressed or anxious. Do something to reduce her conflict, and help her feel more comfortable about what's happening. In the case of our Laund-ur-Mutt™ dog, we suggested the owner towel-dry his dog rather than using the blow dryer. For Coral, we created a very specific routine for putting on her harness, so she knows exactly where to stand and we make certain to put the harness on using the exact same motions every time. This made the event more predictable for her, and less anxiety-producing.

Communication is a Two Way Street

I love watching dogs. I think it's fascinating to see how they communicate with each other. I wish I knew the precise meaning of every subtle cue dogs transmit to each other. We can tell communication has happened when one dog changes its behavior in response to something it read in another's body language that we might not have even seen.

The same thing happens when our dogs watch us. They may see something in our behavior that has meaning to them that we weren't even aware we were doing. Dogs are probably much more careful observers of our body language than we are of theirs.

Learn More

If this chapter has motivated you to learn more about how your dog communicates, we'd highly recommend our Canine Body Postures DVD. While the examples are from professional settings – veterinary clinics, animal shelters, etc. – all the information is just as applicable to you as a dog owner.

Summary

In this chapter you've learned about six features of your dog's body that will help you recognize signs of fear, anxiety and uncertainty in your dog. What if you never knew when your children, spouse, or friends were upset or scared? Their behaviors might seem inappropriate, unpredictable or just "off" because you wouldn't know WHY they were behaving differently. Have you ever had those thoughts about your dog's behavior? It might be because you didn't know your dog was anxious or fearful. Now you have the tools to know.

One of the biggest sources of fear and anxiety for our dogs is the misuse of punishment. That's the subject of our next chapter.

Resources Mentioned in This Chapter

Canine Body Postures: The Professional's Video Guide to Canine Body Language

http://www.animalbehaviorassociates.com/program-canine-behavior-posture.htm

References

* More information about Dr. Michele Wan's research http://www.plosone.org/article/info%3Adoi%2F10.1371%2F journal.pone.0051775

The links to all of the references and resources listed in this book can also be accessed from www.TerribleDogTrainingMistakes.com

Chapter 10: "Because I Said So"

The Mistake: Relying on punishment to change your dog's behavior AND using it incorrectly

How many times have you told your kids "because I said so!"? How many times did you hear it from your parents? I remember hearing it from my dad A LOT when I was growing up. Or maybe he didn't say it all that much, but I remember it because it made such an impression on me. I HATED hearing him say those words to me. First, I knew I wasn't going to be able to do what I wanted to do OR I had to do something I didn't want to do. Second, I can remember thinking, especially as I got a bit older, that because he said so wasn't a good enough reason. But third, I knew if I didn't do what my father wanted, some sort of discipline would follow.

I've had clients tell me "I don't punish him, I just hit him on the nose!" These folks think that "punishment" means something horrible, and since they don't do horrible things to their dogs, they aren't using punishment.

Punishment is defined not by how unpleasant it is, but by its effect on behavior. By definition, punishment is something unpleasant that follows a behavior and decreases its frequency. If you've repeatedly tried to get your dog to stop a behavior to no avail, then by definition what you've been doing isn't punishment. That means it's time to try another approach, because what you've been doing isn't working.

The Reasons People Rely on Punishment and Why This is a Mistake

Default Thinking

You probably don't tell your dog "because I said so", but chances are your default way of thinking when you want your dog's behavior to change is "how can I get him to stop?" That just seems to be human nature. Any time you're thinking about how to suppress behavior, you're likely thinking in terms of punishment. Instead, train your default way of thinking to be "how can I get him to do what I want so I can reward him". We'll talk more about how best to do that in the next chapter "You Want Me To Do What?"

Using Punishment in Anger

Research in child abuse has found that when punishment becomes abusive, it's almost always because it was delivered when parents were angry. It only makes sense the same thing is true when it's used on dogs. It requires a well-thought-out plan to use punishment effectively and humanely. You'll see this VERY clearly when you read the seven rules for effective punishment below. And that's not even all the rules behaviorists have discovered, only the most important ones.

Not Knowing What Else To Do

When calling me for help, dog owners would often tell me, "I've tried everything and I just don't know what else to do!" Many folks don't understand the power of positive reinforcement and how it can be used effectively to change behavior. You might think that using positive reinforcement is bribing your dog, or you always have to have a treat in your hand to get your dog to do what you want. I'll debunk these myths in the next chapter.

Not Recognizing the "Fallout" Punishment Can Cause

If you notice your dog showing a particular behavior less often as the result of you punishing him, it's easy to see why you would conclude punishment "works". Aversive consequences may indeed suppress behavior. But what you might not see immediately are behavior changes such as fear, aggression, your dog avoiding you, or not wanting to do what you want in other circumstances. You also may have been missing the signs of fear and anxiety you now know about after reading the last chapter.

Limitations of Punishment

The best resolution for behavior problems is when a dog learns another behavior that is better for him and acceptable to you. Punishment doesn't teach new behaviors. At best, it only suppresses unwanted ones. It's not just that you want to stop your dog from biting, you want him to be friendly and not want to bite. Suppressing biting doesn't teach your dog how to be friendly. You'll need to do more than punish to accomplish that.

Criteria for the Effective and Humane Use of Punishment

If you expect to use punishment effectively AND humanely (meaning no behavioral or physical harm comes to your dog as a result) you must adhere to certain criteria. I didn't make these criteria up. Instead, they are the results of decades of research about the use of punishment in both people and animals. Once you read them, you'll understand why it's difficult to use appropriately. This is one reason why well informed trainers, behaviorists, behavior consultants and other pet professionals don't rely on punishment much these days.

1. Punishment must be immediate.

Have you ever seen the Gary Larson cartoon with the dog in the front yard with a dynamite detonator, getting ready to push the plunger? The husband and wife are watching from the front window, and she tells her husband that the dog is trying to blow up the house again. She admonishes her husband that he's got to correct him, and "catch him in the act or he'll never learn". No behaviorist worth their salt can give a lecture without including at least one Gary Larson cartoon!

Researchers discovered decades ago that a delay of 3 seconds between the punishment and the behavior significantly reduced the degree to which the punishment suppressed the behavior. Think about the last time you tried to punish your dog for unwanted behavior. Did you make it under 3 seconds? Unless your punishment was yelling at your dog, or maybe using a leash and collar, chances are you didn't have a chance of meeting the deadline.

Because interactive punishment - meaning delivered by you - rarely meets the immediacy rule, it's often better to use startling but harmless "booby traps" if you are using punishment at all. We mentioned the use of devices that are triggered by your dog's own behavior in Chapter 8.

These include the Scat Mat™ , a vinyl mat that delivers a harmless static shock when touched, and the SSSCat, a motion detector that emits an innocuous spray when activated.

2. Punishment must be consistent.

If you want punishment to work, you must catch every single occurrence of the unwanted behavior you want to suppress. How realistic do you think that is? Obviously, it depends on the behavior. But if even a small percentage of the unwanted behavior goes without punishment, it's not going to have the effect you want. Your dog is likely to "gamble" that punishment won't occur.

Let's say you are able to catch your dog about the half the time when she's counter surfing and squirt her with water. The other half of the time, her counter time is rewarded by being able to grab a piece of leftover food. How effective do you think your squirt bottle will be? Not very, because getting on the counter has a 50-50 chance of a big payoff.

As I said in Chapter 8 what often happens with punishment you try to deliver, is that your dog learns not to do the behavior in your presence, but continues to do what you don't want him to do when you aren't around.

3. The unwanted behavior can't be reinforced before punishment occurs.

If your dog can reap the benefits of an unwanted behavior, it will be more likely to continue, despite punishment. If you are quick enough to catch your dog before he jumps on a visitor and is petted for his efforts, your punishment will be much more effective. If however, your dog jumps up, and your visitor pets him, even briefly, and THEN you scold him, your scolding will have little effect on his jumping behavior. In this example, jumping up is also internally rewarded. It *feels good* to your dog to jump up and release tension, so you've already got at least one strike against you by trying to stop jumping with punishment.

4. If you punish one behavior, you must reinforce an alternative behavior if at all possible.

Punishment for one behavior is more effective if you at the same time reinforce another behavior that allows your dog to get what he wants. You'll see much better results if your dog is petted and played with when he keeps all four feet on the ground when greeting visitors while you also prevent jumping up. We talked about the importance of response prevention Chapter 6 "Practice Makes Perfect".

5. The punishment must stop when the unwanted behavior stops.

Let's say your dog jumps up on the table to sneak a piece of pizza (this happened to a friend of ours!). You walk into the room, see your dog on the table and start screaming at him. He jumps down, runs down the hall and hides under the bed, with you close behind, still screaming. What behaviors are being punished now? Certainly not jumping on the table! As soon as your dog jumped down, you should have stopped yelling. Of course, if your dog had already helped himself to several bites of pizza, Rule 3 was already violated, making your yelling much less effective.

6. Punishment must be delivered at the minimum intensity required to stop the behavior.

This is a tricky requirement because either what you do won't be unpleasant enough to stop the behavior OR it will be so unpleasant you'll cause other problems. Let's say you start by quietly telling your dog "No" for jumping up and he repeatedly ignores you. Your dog is learning to ignore you as your voice gradually gets louder. With this pattern, chances are yelling may never stop the jumping.

If instead the first time your dog jumps up on someone, you decide to set off the smoke alarm, he might be frightened enough so that he would never jump again. I'm not recommending this by **ANY** means, because not only would it be extremely difficult to get the timing right, but you also risk the very real danger of creating all sorts of conditioned fears - fear of being near the door, fear of anyone coming inside, and a sensitivity to any loud noise.

The point I'm trying to make is that the smoke alarm is a much more intense noise than you saying NO, and therefore would have a better chance of suppressing the jumping up quickly.

7. Limit the number of applications of a punisher.

If you choose to try punishment, your goal should be to administer it just a few times – some behaviorists recommend no more than 3 to 5 applications. If this does not result in your dog stopping the unwanted behavior, something is wrong. Either punishment isn't the best way to change the behavior (often the case), or you haven't used it correctly (at a minimum you have to follow these seven rules).

Another Option

What you might not know is that there are really two kinds of punishment. What we've been talking about is what behaviorists call "positive punishment". It's not called "positive" because it's good, but because you are **adding** something unpleasant as a behavioral consequence.

Instead, the second type of punishment takes away something your dog wants. If your dog pulls on the leash, you could STOP and stand still. Pulling results in your dog NOT being able to move forward, which is what he wants. This "take-away" method is called negative punishment because what you've done is **subtracted** (taken away) what your dog wants.

The take-away method is less risky as far as creating other behavior problems, BUT it's only useable under certain conditions. Namely, you must be able to control what your dog wants. That's doable in the case of moving forward on a leash. It's not doable if your dog is barking to make passersby leave his territory. The same criteria apply to using negative punishment as for positive punishment. It might be hard to see how rule number 6 applies. Let me give you an example.

One type of negative punishment is called a "time-out from reinforcement". This means you take away any chance of the dog being able to be rewarded for a short time. If your dog jumps on someone, you might put him in a nearby powder room near the front door for a few minutes. If you forget and leave him in there for 10 minutes, the duration, or we could interpret it as the intensity of the "take-away" is too high. Time-outs that are too long have two main problems. First, the likelihood of another unwanted behavior occurring (tearing up the toilet paper) increases. Second, after a relatively brief time, the time-out is no longer relevant or associated with the misbehavior because too much time has passed.

My Best Advice

Whether or not to use any sort of punishment on dogs has become a very divisive topic in the dog behavior and training field. As with most disagreements, the extremes at either end of the spectrum (primarily punishment- and intimidation-based training at one end, and holding that using even a harmless booby trap is inappropriate) may not best serve you.

Relying on punishment to change behavior is a risky business. To do right by your dog and not cause harm, at the very least, you really have to think about whether you can follow the seven rules I've explained. I know from experience that doing so will immediately limit your use of punishment.

Second, suppressing behavior often comes with all kinds of fall-out. Unless and until you limit your dog's opportunities to do what you don't want (which we talked about in

Chapter 6 "Practice Makes Perfect") AND come up with a plan for teaching your dog what you WANT him to do (the subject of the next chapter "You Want Me To Do What?") spending time thinking about how to best punish your dog is not a good use of training time.

If you want to learn more about how your dog learns, and the effective use of rewards and punishment, I recommend two resources. The first is our 5 session webinar course on <u>Fundamentals of Animal Learning</u>. You'll drastically increase your effectiveness in getting your dog to do what you want when you understand these principles

The second resource is a book written by my good friend and colleague Dr. Pamela Reid ***Excel Erated Learning: Explaining in Plain English How Dogs Learn and How Best to Teach Them***. Dr. Reid has done a fantastic job translating quite complex topics in animal learning into language anyone can understand.

Summary

In this chapter you learned about seven criteria necessary for the appropriate use of punishment. Meeting these criteria means that if you are considering using punishment (especially positive punishment) to change your dog's behavior, you need to have a well- thought-out plan.

Exploding in anger after your dog misbehaves is almost a guarantee you won't meet the necessary criteria.

You also learned about negative punishment, or the "take-away" method which can be quite effective for changing some behaviors. This type of punishment has several additional criteria that must be met for effective use.

Finally you learned to be wary of the extreme views on this topic that are prevalent in the dog training and behavior world.

Resources Mentioned in this Chapter

Fundamentals of Animal Learning Webinar Course
http://petprowebinars.com/courses-by-instructor/fundamentals-of-animal-learning/

Excel Erated Learning: Explaining in Plain English How Dogs Learn and How Best to Teach Them
http://www.dogwise.com/ItemDetails.cfm?ID=DTB500&AffiliateID=45232&Method=3

The Scat Mat™

http://store.petsafe.net/scatmat-medium-30-x16

The SSSCat® - http://www.amazon.com/Ssscat-PDT00-13914-SSSCAT-Cat-

Training/dp/B000RIA95G/ref=sr_1_1?ie=UTF8&qid=13967
60919&sr=8-1&keywords=ssscat+spray

The links to all of the references and resources listed in this book can also be accessed from www.TerribleDogTrainingMistakes.com

Chapter 11: You Want Me To Do What?

The Mistake: Failing to reinforce good behavior.

When you receive good service from a company, how often do you take the time to write a letter thanking the service provider and commending the company on a job well done? Unless you had an extraordinary experience, my prediction is you've written very few of these letters. I know I haven't, I'm ashamed to admit. It's uncommon for any of us to go out of our way, other than perhaps to say 'thank-you', to reward good behavior.

On the other hand, I'm much more likely to fire off a nasty letter or email if a company failed to live up to my expectations.

I found myself having to hold back from doing just that recently when a product I ordered took three weeks to arrive. Turns out the company had shipped it to my billing address rather than the mailing address I provided. I was willing to overlook that – mistakes happen. But what really annoyed me was the company's failure to give me feedback on the status of my package. I was forced to constantly email them and ask for updates. It was like pulling teeth to try to get any information out of them.

This natural human tendency to notice, and comment on, bad behavior, while ignoring good behavior because we just expect it to occur, is one of the terrible twelve training mistakes when applied to our dogs.

Why This Is a Mistake

We've already talked about the dangers of focusing on punishment as the primary or best way to train your dog or change his behavior. The other side of the coin is that if you don't give your dog enough feedback about his good behavior, it will be harder for him to figure it out on his own. Granted, avoiding a bad consequence is a type of reinforcement, but being given something good is a much better idea!

Ashley and the Hallway

Behavior that is reinforced increases in frequency. Let me give you an example. We acquired our last Dalmatian, Ashley, as a four-month-old puppy. Ashley had been abandoned in Gunnison Colorado, a small mountain community in southwest Colorado. A friend of ours and fellow Dalmatian owner discovered Ashley was in the animal shelter and suggested we come meet her. To make a long story short, we adopted Ashley.

From her very first day with us, Ashley was a challenge. She was never still unless she was asleep. I came out of the bathroom one day to find Ashley lying quietly in the hallway outside the bathroom door. I was so thrilled she wasn't being her typical whirling dervish self, I spent some time petting and talking to her. Later that evening, I came out of the bathroom to again find Ashley lying in the hall. I delivered more attention. Within just a few days, this became a regular pattern. As a result of spontaneously catching Ashley lying down and rewarding her for it, I caused that behavior to rapidly become a habit.

Why We Forget to Reward Good Behavior

It's easy to ignore your dog if she isn't in trouble and is behaving nicely. This is especially true for youngsters like Ashley was when we first acquired her. You're so busy dealing with puppy behaviors – chewing, nipping, housetraining, and more – that when your puppy is lying quietly you just breathe a sigh of relief rather than reward her for that behavior.

You might also be worried that if you pay attention to your dog when she's quiet, she'll get excited and jump up, nip, or do the other things you don't want her to do. While there is a slight risk of that with very excitable dogs and young puppies, all you need to do is walk away again. Your dog will quickly learn, as Ashley did, that staying quiet is what causes you to keep the attention coming. Overexuberant behavior causes you to go away.

Your Dog Needs To Know What You Want

As another example, we just had a new logo designed for our membership site Behavior Education Network (as of this writing, it may or may not be active on the site!) I showed it to our members via our Facebook group. I needed our members' feedback about the logo. I needed to know if they liked the logo or they didn't. If I didn't ask them, I might choose a new logo that our members hated. Then I'd hear about it for sure.

Your dog also needs to know what you like. If you don't tell her, she's left on her own to choose a behavior in a particular situation. And you can bet you'll tell her about it if she picks the wrong one. So make it easy on you and on your dog, and start to proactively catch and reward your dog for good behavior.

How to Establish a New Habit of Reinforcing Good Behavior

In order to get in the habit of giving your dog more feedback about good behavior, your homework is to identify five behaviors you can reward your dog for every single day. The more rewards you give, the quicker you'll see these behaviors occur more often. My prediction is that you'll discover several unexpected benefits from this technique.

First, you'll begin to like your dog even more than you already do. You'll see how fast she can learn. You'll enjoy rewarding her. As her behaviors improve and she does more and more of what you want, you'll be reminded of how great it is to have her be part of your family.

Second, as the behaviors you want increase in frequency, behaviors you haven't reinforced will naturally decrease. There's only so many hours in the day. If your dog is doing more of what you want (lying quietly) there is less time available for her to do what you don't want (running crazily around the house!). That's exactly what happened with Ashley. The more consistent I became remembering to pet Ashley when she was lying quietly, the more often I found her doing just that. Her time spent in "hyper mode" began to decrease. Progress!!!

After you're seeing substantially more of the first five behaviors you've chosen from your dog, choose another five to reinforce. After three or four go-rounds of this technique, you'll be amazed at the change in your dog's pattern of behaviors.

What's Reinforcing?

Petting Ashley was not the only reinforcement I used. In fact, petting is often not a very powerful reinforcer because most dogs get petted a LOT, for no particular reason. If your relationship with your dog is unbalanced, and she's not getting much attention from you, petting and social contact may be more important than usual.

I think petting worked well for Ashley as a reinforcer in the beginning, because she'd been deprived of social contact during her time on the streets in Gunnison.

Especially when first helping your dog to acquire a new behavior through reinforcement, the more irresistible your reinforcement, the more successful you'll be. Food, petting, and the chance to play with either you or a toy are typically good reinforcers for most dogs, especially in the way I'm talking about using them in this chapter.

A Related Tip

Even though we aren't talking in this chapter about how to teach your dog to sit, down, or come, those are some of the five daily behaviors you might catch your dog doing that you will reinforce. Let me give you a tip about teaching those behaviors that all good trainers and behaviorists know, but many pet owners don't.

When you are first teaching your dog to sit, you might lure him into position by holding a treat over his head. Do NOT start saying "Sit, Sit, Sit" at this point. Your dog doesn't yet know what behavior to "attach" to that word. Instead, wait to add the word Sit (what trainers call a cue) until your dog is almost always putting himself into a sit when he sees your hand with the treat over his head. That's when you want to say "Sit" about the same time (or a fraction of a second before) your hand comes out. The next step is to say "Sit", and wait for a second before bringing out your hand. That's the point at which the signal for sitting gets transferred, so to speak, from your hand and the treat, to the word "Sit".

Truth Be Told

To be honest, my catching and rewarding Ashley for lying down in the hallway didn't precisely follow the "rules" for using positive reinforcement. I should have started petting her as soon as she lay down, because like punishment, reinforcement should immediately follow a behavior. I don't know how long Ashley had been lying in the hallway when I came out of the bathroom. It couldn't have been very long because I wasn't "indisposed" for very long!

Maybe what she was learning was that "good things happen to me when Mom comes out of the bathroom, so I'll lie here and wait for her". It doesn't matter. It worked for both of us – Ashley got petted and I got a dog who quietly lay down more often.

Learning More

My purpose in this chapter is to point out how important it is to give your dog more feedback for good behavior than she is receiving now. You'll have a good start by following through with the homework I gave you, but there's a lot more you should know about making the most of positive reinforcement to change your dog's behavior.

Delving into the details is beyond the scope of this book – after all, we are talking about mistakes. But there are a plethora of books that provide the instruction and detail you need, and I've listed my recommendations at the end of this chapter. I'd recommend getting at least one from that list and learn more about using positive reinforcement. If you've been mostly of the "because I said so" mind set, you'll discover an entirely different way of getting your dog to do what you want. Focusing on how to get your dog to do what you want so you can reinforce good behavior is without a doubt the best approach to dog training.

Summary

In this chapter you learned the importance of giving your dog more feedback for good behavior. Too many dogs get most of their information about their behaviors when their owners are unhappy with them, and not nearly enough information when they are behaving appropriately. Sometimes dogs learn what to do and not do because the behaviors you like don't cause anything bad to happen (they are too often ignored). Sort of a "no news is good news" approach to training your dog. That's not a very enjoyable way to learn. It takes a lot of joy out of life.

Get started on identifying the five behaviors from your dog you are going to reinforce every day. If there are absolutely no behaviors your dog shows (I don't believe that for a second!) that you can reward, you really do need immediate professional help for your dog's behavior. I say that both in jest and in all seriousness. You can use the information in the bonus chapter 13 to evaluate who to work with.

When you begin reinforcing good behavior more often, it's important your entire family is on the same page about what good behavior is. That's the subject of our next and almost final chapter "Make Up Your Minds".

Additional Resources

Behavior Education Network

http://www.BehaviorEducationNetwork.com

Family Friendly Dog Training – A Six Week Program for You and Your Dog by Patricia McConnell and Aimee Moore

Print Book

http://www.dogwise.com/ItemDetails.cfm?ID=DTB917&AffiliateID=45232&Method=3

E-Book
http://www.dogwise.com/ItemDetails.cfm?ID=DTB917EBK&AffiliateID=45232&Method=3

Excel Erated Learning: Explaining in Plain English How Dogs Learn and How Best to Teach Them by Pamela Reid
Print Book –

http://www.dogwise.com/ItemDetails.cfm?ID=DTB500&AffiliateID=45232&Method=3

E-Book
http://www.dogwise.com/ItemDetails.cfm?ID=DTB500EBK&AffiliateID=45232&Method=3

How to Behave So Your Dog Behaves, 2nd Edition by Sophia Yin

Print Book

http://www.dogwise.com/ItemDetails.cfm?ID=DTB807&AffiliateID=45232&Method=3

E-Book -

http://www.dogwise.com/ItemDetails.cfm?ID=DTB807EBK&AffiliateID=45232&Method=3

The links to all of the references and resources listed in this book can also be accessed from www.TerribleDogTrainingMistakes.com

Chapter 12: Make Up Your Minds!

The Mistake: Inconsistencies and disagreements in the family about what is acceptable behavior for your dog.

When Dan and I first moved in together about 25 years ago, I had three dogs. I had shown all three dogs in obedience competitions, earning 3 titles on two of them and two on the third dog. I was very much in a trainer's mindset at that time with my dogs. What I mean by that is there were certain things I wanted to be very consistent about with my dogs. I'll tell you exactly what those were a little later.

Although he grew up with dogs and his parents still had a dog, Dan had not had a dog of his own as an adult. Although he's a behaviorist and worked with many different species of animals, he'd never trained a dog.

In addition, both of us were under quite a bit of stress when we first blended our households of my three dogs and 2 cats, and his 2 cats. I had moved cross-country to where he was teaching at a large university. We'd both moved several times in the previous few years, as both of us experienced divorces. I was in a completely new environment – where Dan lived in the southeastern part of the U.S. is much different from the Rocky Mountain west, where I'd lived all my life.

His cats, I'm sure, thought the world had come to an end, as they now not only had to adapt to a different house, but a totally different social environment. My dogs were accustomed to living with cats, but it had been just me and them for awhile, so they were now adjusting to another person sharing time with their mom.

What do you think the chances were that we would immediately be on the same page when it came to managing our expanded pet household? You guessed it – slim and none. A lot of compromise and negotiation had to take place immediately. Let me give you a few examples.

The Issues

Here are a few of the more important examples of how Dan and I were not on the same page about the dogs when we first combined households.

- I had taught the dogs that "Down" meant lie down while "Off" meant get off the furniture or "off" of me (although the dogs rarely jumped on anyone, as I'd been quite strict about that). Dan tended to use "Down" or "Get Down" for both actions. That drove me crazy.

- If I needed to do something mildly unpleasant to the dogs – clip their nails, look in their ears, or give them a pill – I would always go to them. I never called them to me, as I'd been taught coming when called should *always* result in nothing but a good experience. Dan, on the other hand, would call a dog to him for those very reasons. Sigh.

- I religiously tried to avoid using the dogs' names as a stand-alone "command". In other words, I wouldn't just say "Blaze", without following her name with what I wanted her to do. I wasn't perfect, but I'd usually catch myself if I just said a name without something following, like "Come". Dan would often say just the dogs' names alone when he wanted them to come. I'd often follow that up with "Well what do you want them to do?", which would annoy him no end.

- Dan didn't want the dogs in the kitchen at all. Nor did he want them to be able to sleep in the bedroom. Neither of us wanted them on the bed, but I thought the dogs should be pretty much allowed in any room of the house.

Potential Effects on Our Dogs

If both Dan and I had continued dealing with the dogs in our very different ways, and setting different "rules" for them, can you imagine how confused they would have become? What would it have been like for them if sometimes when they were in the kitchen it was no big deal, but 10 minutes later they got yelled at for the very same thing? Or if one was lying on the couch and Dan said "get down", the dog would think "Huh? I already am lying down! What do you want me to do?"

You can probably see the parallels with children, if you are parents. People have different opinions, desires, and beliefs about what family relationships ought to look like. And your relationship with your dog is a family relationship that will need to be negotiated just like any other.

Not only did our different views confuse the dogs, it also produced ongoing conflict between the two of us. Dan didn't appreciate my reminding him (nagging is the term I think he used!) about what to say and not say to the dogs, and I was annoyed that he wasn't doing what the dogs were accustomed to. I thought they'd been through enough upheaval by moving across the country, and the more their daily routine resembled what they'd grown to expect, the easier the adjustment would be for them. Dan didn't disagree with me, but keeping life consistent for the dogs meant he had to learn some new habits. I also had to learn to be a bit more flexible, and we both had to compromise.

What We Did

Getting on the same page with the dogs didn't happen overnight. It was a gradual process, although there were some issues we needed to compromise on immediately. We decided for example, that the dogs could not be in the kitchen during meal preparation. They particularly bothered Dan if they were underfoot when we were scurrying around trying to get food on the table. It would be OK for them to be in the kitchen if we went in to get a snack or something to drink.

I learned to be less strict with the "down" versus "off" issue and stopped saying anything to Dan if he used "down" for either. But I held firm on his not calling the dogs to do something unpleasant to them. He was willing to work on learning to do that.

We agreed the dogs could be in the bedroom until we turned out the lights to go to sleep. Then we put up a baby gate to keep them out. We gave them comfortable dog beds in several rooms in the house. Plus, since they pretty much had the run of the house at night, they could sleep on whatever couch or chair they wanted to.

What You Can Do

Unless you've specifically sat the family down and talked about it, chances are not all of your family members are on the same page when it comes to your dog. Your differences might involve more substantial issues than Dan and I encountered, or you might have just small details you need to work out.

Either way, it's time to plan a family meeting to come to an agreement about the important guidelines for your dog's behavior.

Make a List

Start by making a list of the areas in which there is disagreement now. Under each item, describe each family member's views or habits. Dad wants the dogs to sleep on the bed, Mom doesn't. Mom says "come here sweetie pie", but Dad says "GET OVER HERE", when he wants the dog to come, even when he's not mad at the dog! You may or may not be able to tackle every item on the list during one meeting. It depends on how long your list is and how big the differences of opinion are!

When to Have the Conversation

Choose a time to talk about the dog when everyone is in a good mood. Don't do it after you've just had a disagreement about the dog's behavior, when Dad is trying to watch a football game, or Mom is trying to get out the door for a run. Know going into the conversation that everyone will have to compromise.

Be Specific

Notice how specific Dan and I were in defining what was acceptable and what wasn't. When the dogs could be in the kitchen and the bedroom and when they couldn't. The more concrete you can be, the easier it will be for everyone to follow the guidelines and the less confused your dog will be.

Display Your Results

Put the list of what your family has agreed on in several prominent places. This is a proactive way to prevent disagreements about what everyone agreed to. If you have a particularly contentious set of circumstances, you could even require everyone to put their initials at the end of the document. That way someone can't claim they never agreed to what's on the list. This may seem a bit extreme, but I've seen some really nasty family arguments over the dog. Once everyone has agreed to a plan – even if everyone isn't completely happy about all of it – then it's much more likely both human and dog behavior will change for the better.

Be Aware of Baggage

It is VERY common for disagreements about your dog to be a reflection of other discord in the family. You may know exactly what I'm talking about, or this might be something you'd not thought of before. I learned about this in my days of working with the pet loss support program at Colorado State University's Veterinary Teaching Hospital. I was one of the co-founders of the program, along with colleagues, who became close friends, from the marriage and family therapy department. Sometimes, the more important underlying family issues are too scary to confront, so they get played out instead in other contexts – such as disagreements about the dog's behavior. Two warning signs that this may be the case:

1. If despite what you feel is everyone's best efforts, there are one or more issues about your dog that your family just can't agree on, or arrive at some compromise about

2. Your discussion sounds like ground hog day – you are just having the same argument over and over again – with no one budging an inch

Resolving conflicts within the family is way beyond the scope of this chapter, or of what I'm qualified to help with. But those may be signs that the issue is bigger than your dog. At the very least, try to arrive at some small agreements about your dog.

Set a Time to Re-Evaluate

Once you agree on a plan, get everyone's commitment to try it for a set time period. A week is a good starting point. Set a time at the end of the meeting to get together to discuss how the new plan is working. Chances are, you'll have to do several rounds of tweaking before you arrive at decisions that will work for everyone. This would also be a good reason to meet with a certified behaviorist or trainer. That person can help you look at your plan and your guidelines from your dog's point of view to see if your expectations are reasonable.

Flash Forward

For us, things have changed quite a bit in the 25 or so years we've been together. I no longer show my dogs in competition so I'm more flexible about what I expect from them. After working as the animal behaviorist at a large, very well-known animal shelter, and working with probably a thousand or more pet owners, my priorities have changed about what's important for dogs to do and not do. Dan now has many years of experience living with dogs and better understands why I was such a stickler about certain things years ago.

We rarely have disagreements about our dogs now. In any family or relationship, many aspects of life need to be negotiated and compromises made. How your dog fits into your family is just one of many.

Summary

In this chapter I gave you specific steps for how to arrive at agreements about what's acceptable and not acceptable behavior for your dog. You also leaned the problems that can occur not only with your dog, but within your family, if everyone isn't in agreement. And I listed several warning signs of when differences of opinion may really not be about the dog at all.

This chapter was really about how important it is for your family members to communicate about your dog's behavior.

Bonus Chapter: Whisperers Need Not Apply

The Mistake: Being confused by the alphabet soup of credentials in the dog training and behavior field, not knowing how to evaluate a service provider, falling victim to outrageous claims, guarantees or charismatic personnas, and still not finding the best person who will do right by you and your dog.

Even though I'm calling this a mistake, I don't want to imply that this, or any of the other mistakes in this book, is your fault. It's a confusing world out there! You've probably seen all kinds of initials after a person's name, and you have no way of knowing what they are unless you ask. AND, you have to know what questions to ask to get answers that will really help you evaluate the person you're considering hiring. Notice I said hiring.

Don't Expect Free

There's an enormous amount of free information on the web about pet behavior and training. Tons of blogs and forums, non-profit sites, and businesses. Some of the best free information can be found at the ASPCA's Virtual Pet Behaviorist site (in addition of course to the large number of articles on our websites!).

But if you are calling people who have behavior and training businesses, do not expect them to give you advice over the phone for free. I can't tell you how many times someone has called and said "I just have a quick question", and then want to tell me a long story about a complex behavior problem. There is no way that could be a quick question, and the dog's problem is certainly not going to have a quick solution.

"Quick fixes" often aren't the right, or the best solutions. Aside from general recommendations that could do no harm – such as keeping dogs that are fighting separated for now, or not allowing the untrained puppy into the room she's been urinating in – off the cuff advice could be just the wrong thing to do and serve to worsen your dog's behavior.

Personalized and customized help for your dog won't come free. I'm not even going to try giving examples of fee schedules, because not only would that not be a good thing for me to do legally, but also because there is tremendous variation.

Fees vary dramatically in different parts of the country (any trainer or behaviorist in New York City for example, is going to cost more than in Pueblo, Colorado). Individuals with advanced degrees (Ph.D. or DVM) also tend to charge more than someone without. Someone just starting their business may tend to charge less than the average rate for comparable services in the area.

The bottom line for you though, is that fee doesn't always correlate well with the quality of the service. You won't necessarily get the best from the highest price person, nor the worst from the least expensive. There are many more important criteria to pay attention to.

Start with the Right Mindset

Searching for someone to help you with your dog's training or behavior problem is something you have to take seriously. You want your *children's* teacher to be well educated and professionally trained – not just someone who loves children and likes to teach. If your child was having behavior or learning problems in school you'd seek out a counselor or psychologist who was professionally educated and trained.

Seek out help for your dog from the same perspective. Your dog is going to be a part of your family for likely well over 10 years so investing in the best help available is worth it. Your dog's well-being – and even his life – may literally depend on getting the right help.

If someone else referred you to a person, that's a good sign. But you still must do your homework. Just because the individual was a good fit for someone else doesn't automatically mean their services will be what your dog needs.

Terminology

There is no licensing for dog trainers or behavior consultants in the U.S., so anyone can use any professional title they choose. Just because someone calls themselves a "behaviorist" doesn't mean they've had any formal education in the science of animal behavior. Remember from the Introduction, that I reserve the term "behaviorist" for someone who has a graduate degree in a behavioral science, or a veterinarian who has completed a behavior residency (which may or may not include a post-graduate behavior degree). Non-degreed people will still label themselves "behaviorists" but I use the term "behavior consultant" or variation. Some individuals even use "behavior therapist" (a term which in some states may be illegal because the "therapist" designation is a term protected through state licensing).

My own bias is that I believe it's a questionable practice to call oneself a "behaviorist" without an advanced degree in a behavioral science or at least a veterinary behavioral residency. That would send up a red flag to me that someone was trying to appear to "pad" their resume or credentials a bit. Trainers should be willing, and proud, to stand on their own laurels. Good, competent trainers are priceless and have developed great hands-on skills working with dogs. They should be proud of that instead of using a professional term that doesn't accurately describe their background. If the person is willing to fudge on this issue, who knows what else s/he will be willing to be less than honest about?

Evaluate Credentials

With all the credentials available to dog trainers today, you should be wary of anyone who doesn't hold any credentials at all. But all credentials are not created equal. Credentials that come from private, for profit dog training schools, or academies, or other entities (some even call themselves colleges although they are in no way comparable to a four year accredited college of higher learning) only mean the person has satisfactorily completed the required curriculum.

Credentials that come from independent professional organizations require some sort of criteria or standard to be met before the credential is awarded. This should include at least educational and experiential criteria. Only two credentials require advanced degrees. Certified Applied (or Associate) Animal Behaviorists must have a Ph.D. (or Master's degree) in a behavioral science. Veterinary behaviorists must be DVMs, but are not required to hold an advanced degree in a behavioral science (although they must complete a residency and a certification examination).

Some credentials also require passing a test, letters of recommendation from peers and/or colleagues, or reviews of case histories by the certifying board. Some also require continuing education, or some other type of evidence that the person is staying current in the field.

Other credentials certify the applicant to deliver or present a specific presentation or training protocol a particular business has claimed as its own. Someone could be certified in training protocol ABC or to work with a specialized audience or problem such as kids and dogs or dog-dog aggression, or any number of possibilities. There seem to be more of these cropping up. Although perhaps not politically correct, to be honest, my insider tip is to not give much weight to these types of credentials. Anyone who holds a legitimate credential that requires sufficient education and experience should have sufficient knowledge to work with the audience or problem.

If you don't know what the letters after a person's name stand for, you'll need to ask. And you'll also need to ask about what entity awards the credential and what the criteria are. If the person is reluctant to tell you or seems annoyed that you would ask, that should be a red flag.

I'm proud of my credential of Certified Applied Animal Behaviorist and would love for anyone to learn more about it at the Animal Behavior Society's website.

Rather than asking the person to provide details about their certification, you could just ask for the website address so you can review the credential more completely.

Below is my suggestion for a checklist of the questions to ask about whatever certification credential the individual holds.

Crucial Questions to Ask About a Credential

- What is the certifying body or entity? How long has it been in existence?
- What are the educational criteria for certification? Is a college or post-graduate degree required?
- Are there experiential requirements? Is the successful applicant required to have a certain amount of supervised or unsupervised experience in the field? Is the experience evaluated in some way

through case histories, direct observation or review of videos?

- Is any testing required? How was the test created? Who created the questions, and what process was used? Who administers the test? Test questions should meet certain statistical and validity criteria and the testing process should be supervised to ensure fairness.

- What are the criteria for certification renewal? Look for criteria that indicate the person is keeping current in the field.

More Than Credentials

Credentials are an absolutely necessary first step to evaluate. But because of the variability in credentialing, you'll have to investigate a little further. Some credentialed people routinely make the mistakes you just learned about, although this is much more likely to happen if someone is not credentialed. There are a few key questions you can pose to someone that will reveal rather quickly how much this person knows about the science of behavior and recent developments in the field, versus how much information is "made up", as we talked about in Chapter 8 and the Introduction. These questions will also reveal those who hold the more extreme beliefs about techniques, on both ends of the "positive" and "aversive" spectrum as we talked about in Chapters 7, 10 and 11.

Key Questions to Ask

1. How important is it for me to be "dominant" over my dog? What do I have to do to accomplish that? Do you think the problem I'm calling about is a "dominance problem?"

You'll know what the "right" answers are from reading Chapter 1. You can use a variety of terms in your question, such as pack leadership, alpha status, or pack theory.

2. What sort of collar do you recommend I use?

You've learned that choke chains and pinch collars are not "state of the art", but the person should show some flexibility regarding harnesses and head collars, based on your individual needs and preferences.

3. Do you use food rewards?

You've learned that if people are adamantly opposed to using food, that's likely an indication their knowledge of learning theory isn't up to date.

4. Do you guarantee your results?

185

If the answer is yes, results – meaning solving a particular behavior or training issue – are guaranteed, it's time to say thanks very much, goodbye. Would you expect your doctor or your psychologist, or even your child's teacher to make a guarantee? Of course not! Whatever "guarantee" is offered, read the fine print closely.

5. I'm all for rewarding my dog and focusing on good behavior, but sometimes I need to tell her she can't do something – like getting into the trash. Is it OK to tell her no or to use a harmless "booby-trap"?

This question should help you evaluate whether or not the person's approach is similar to your beliefs and what you've learned in this book. If the answer is something along the lines "your dog needs to obey you / you can't let her get away with anything / put her leash on and give her a "correction", chances are the person is more focused on the "dominance", punitive style of training. On the other hand, if the answer makes you feel as if your dog's problem is your fault or the only options are better management – you shouldn't leave the trash out, you shouldn't have her in contexts that trigger the barking – the person's "toolbox" for helping you, may not be full enough.

Can You Observe?

If you're looking for a class, ask to sit in on one. If someone refuses, I'd be suspicious. It's not as if you are looking to get training or information for free (you wouldn't be bringing your dog). You just want to see if everyone is having a good time, the class is well managed and not too big, and you like the way the person talks to the students – both human and canine!

For confidentiality and safety reasons, it will be unlikely a behavior consultant would allow a pet owner to sit in on a consultation with another client. But you can ask the behaviorist or behavior consultant for references, such as from veterinarians or shelters that use their services, or from former clients who have given permission to share information.

Trust Your Gut

If anyone tells you to do something to or with your dog that you don't feel comfortable with – don't do it! You should not be intimidated, bullied or shamed into doing something you believe is not in the best interest of your dog. You should not allow anyone to work directly with your dog unless the individual first tell you what s/he is going to do. Don't be afraid to tell any trainer or behavior consultant to stop if the person is doing something to your dog you feel is harmful or just not right.

Look for Good Relationships with Veterinarians

Because behavior problems can have medical causes, look for people who want to make sure your veterinarian has evaluated your dog and ruled out medical reasons for the behavior or training issue. You also want someone who is on good terms with your local veterinary community and feels comfortable talking directly with your veterinarian, if you give permission.

Be wary of trainers or behavior consultants who insist on diet changes, make specific recommendations for medication or alternative homeopathic remedies without relying on input from veterinarians.

Common Credentials

Now it's time for you to do your homework. Below, you'll find a list of some of the more common credentials in the dog training and behavior field. I've even supplied the links to give you a head start. Spend some time looking at the websites, the credentialing criteria and how each group positions itself and what claims they make.

I'll be honest here. This is an edited list. There are MANY more certifications, some of which have a greater number of people certified than the groups I've listed. I'll likely get angry letters, bad reviews, and some people won't buy this book because I haven't listed a particular group or organization. But I'm writing this book for you – the dog owner. I'm trying to help you avoid mistakes so why would I list a particular credential that I think could cause you to make a mistake? You can investigate other credentials on your own if you wish.

But I'd recommend starting with the list below first. Then you will at least have a basis for comparison if you run across other credentials you want to know more about.

You might have seen an article or two that attempts to create a hierarchy of credentials. I believe this is totally inappropriate. A Certified Applied Animal Behaviorist isn't better or higher or lower in the "food chain", as one article says, than a Veterinary Behaviorist, or vice versa. Instead, each brings different strengths, education, and experience to the table.

Behaviorists are not better than trainers, but each has a different skill set because of their education and experience. You may need a different type of professional for different behavior and training problems.

Credentialing Groups

Academy for Dog Trainers

https://www.academyfordogtrainers.com/

American College of Veterinary Behaviorists

http://www.dacvb.org/

Animal Behavior Society's Professional Certification

http://www.animalbehavior.org/ABSAppliedBehavior/certifie

d-applied-animal-behaviorists/about-the-program-for-

certified-applied-animal-

behaviorists/?searchterm=Programs

Certification Council of Professional Dog Trainers

www.ccpdt.org/

International Association of Animal Behavior Consultants

https://iaabc.org/about

Karen Pryor Certified Training Partner

https://www.karenpryoracademy.com/about

Summary

In this chapter you learned that evaluating people you are considering hiring to help with your dog's behavior and training issue may not be an easy task. But it's a crucial one, and for your dog's sake, you can't afford to take short cuts. Use the lists I gave you in this chapter, as well as the one in the Conclusion section to find a qualified, competent professional for behavior and training help with your dog.

You can get on the good side of anyone you contact by not expecting free advice, or expecting someone to help you change your dog's behavior overnight.

On the other hand, you deserve a respectful and caring attitude from the behavior or training service provider you choose, and not to be blamed for your dog's behavioral issues. If you expect to have the well behaved dog you want, you must also be willing to commit to implementing a reasonable and appropriate plan the professional creates for you.

Resources Mentioned in this Chapter

ASPCA's Virtual Pet Behaviorist

http://www.aspca.org/pet-care/virtual-pet-behaviorist

Delta Society's *Professional Standards for Dog Trainer: Humane, Effective Principles.*

Provides guidance in identifying humane and effective dog training principles.

http://www.petpartners.org/document.doc?id=374

CONCLUSION

Your Opportunity

Now you know about 12 terrible dog training mistakes. These aren't the only mistakes I've seen dog owners make over the years, but they are the ones I've see most commonly and that are most likely to create the most problems for you and your dog.

If you've made most, or even all of these mistakes, don't beat yourself up about it. Dogs are the most forgiving of creatures. My German Shorthaired Pointer, Brandy, was the first dog I ever trained for obedience competition back in the late 1970s. You saw several pictures of her back in Chapter 9 on canine body language.

I did so many things wrong during Brandy's training. Yet she remained my sweet, friendly companion for almost 16 years. I apologized to her, before she died, for all the things I wished I would have done differently.

Now you have the chance to do things differently. By avoiding these 12 mistakes in the future you and your dog are now repositioned onto the right path for both of you to get what you want out of your relationship with each other.

You can use the following checklist I created for you as a reminder to keep you on track.

Checklist

Use this checklist to remind yourself of twelve actions you should be taking to have a better-behaved dog, a dog that is happier because you now understand her better and are better able to communicate with her, and more prepared to meet her behavioral needs.

Use the checklist as well to keep the entire family on the same page about how best to train your dog. Make sure every family member is able to answer "yes" to each question during your regular family meetings or discussions about your dog's behavior. If any one person is having difficulty saying "yes", you can revisit that chapter in the book. The checklist can also be used as a basis for interviewing a behavior or training professional you want to hire to give you individualized help with your dog.

1. Am I striving to create a relationship with my dog based on good communication and cooperation rather than worrying about dominance?

2. Have I started a regular walking program with my dog – everyday - with weather days off allowed only

for my or my dog's safety?

3. Do I know what steps to take to help my dog calm down when she's afraid, without worrying that by paying attention to her I am making her fear worse?

4. Am I limiting the time my dog spends in a crate or otherwise confined, knowing that excess crating masks problems, and doesn't allow my dog to get her needs met for exercise, play, and social contact?

5. Have I started a behavior management plan so my dog doesn't have the chance to repeat unwanted behaviors over and over again?

6. Have I realized that my dog does NOT know right from wrong, and learned to recognize "guilty looks" for the submissive behaviors they are?

7. Have I started a new habit of NOT allowing my dog to greet other dogs she meets on walks unless she already knows them? Alternatively, if I've decided to allow some meetings, do I know what to look for as a dog approaches so I can choose the ones most likely to go well, and avoid all the rest?

8. Have I had the family meeting, and now have everyone in agreement about the guidelines for our dog's behaviors? Are all family members on board about communicating the same way with your dog?

9. Have I reexamined my use of punishment with my dog, taken steps to minimize its use, and made sure that if I do use it, I am doing so ONLY if I can meet the 7 requirements for its humane and effective use?

10. Have I begun a program of rewarding my dog for a *minimum* of 5 behaviors every day? (You should easily be able to double that number!) Have I identified what types of reinforcement my dog likes the best?

11. Have I committed to NOT ever alpha rolling, pinning or scruff-shaking my dog? Have I decided not to rely on grabbing my dog's collar to control her (except in an emergency?) Have I committed to not prying anything out of her mouth except in an emergency (If your dog counter surfs and "steals" a piece of steak, that does NOT qualify as an emergency! ONLY items that could harm her, not necessarily ones you don't want damaged qualify as

an emergency!).

12. Can I now recognize when my dog is fearful, anxious, or uncertain and know what I can do to relieve her discomfort and emotional distress?

Next Steps

You have so many more resources available to help you continue your dog's education, compared to what I had to choose from at the beginning of my dog training endeavors. I hope you'll continue learning more about your dog by investigating at least one of the additional resources I have listed in the Resource sections at the end of most chapters.

And if you'll be looking for a professional to help you, be SURE you read my guidelines for choosing that person. When you are interviewing people, ask them what they think about one or more of the 12 mistakes you've read about in this book. Avoid anyone who doesn't know what you know after reading this book.

One VERY logical next step is to work on bringing out the best in your dog. We have a webinar course on just that topic – "Bringing Out the Best In Your Dog's Behavior" – and it is the absolute perfect next step for you and your dog. Not only does it give you more in-depth implementation protocols for avoiding some of the mistakes you learned about in this book, you'll also discover a five step plan to help you improve your dog's behavior. Because you've purchased this 12 mistakes book, I'm giving you a 50% on this webinar training, complete with downloadable video and audio presentations and an edited transcript for future reference. You'll pay only $24 for the entire course that regularly sells for $47. It's available at PetProWebinars.com. Type in the coupon code "mistakes" (all lower case) in the shopping cart and your discount will be taken automatically.

Final Thoughts

Avoiding these 12 mistakes in the future requires making some changes in your own behavior, as well as in how you think about your dog, and your attitude toward her. Start doing things differently in whatever area you think is having the most dramatic negative impact on your dog's behavior.

Maybe it's getting her out of the crate, or at least reacclimating her to the crate. Perhaps it's stopping the inappropriate and ineffective attempts at punishment. You have 10 other possibilities to choose from!

I'd like to thank you for reading this book. I believe it speaks to your commitment to your dog. You care enough to take the time to learn about your dog's behavior rather than just doing what you've always done, which admittedly hasn't given you the results you wanted.

I've been privileged to share my home with one or more dogs since I was 5 years old. My life would be much the poorer without sharing all those years with my canine best friends. They've taught me much more than I've ever taught them. I'm grateful I've been given the chance to share some of what they taught me, as well as what I've learned through my training as a behavior scientist, in this book. Now, go fix your mistakes, and enjoy your dog!

Resources

"Bringing Out the Best in Your Dog's Behavior"
http://petprowebinars.com/courses-by-instructor/suzanne-hetts-dan-estep/bring-out-your-dogs-best-behavior-in-five-easy-steps/

For Pet Professionals

1. Leverage What You've Learned

Because you bought my book, I'd like to help you use it to attract new clients and reward your current ones by enhancing the conversations you have with your clients. Trainers have asked me for a book like this for a long time. Trainers who are current in their scientific knowledge about dogs find themselves talking to their clients all the time about some, or all, of these 12 mistakes. Trainers want something they can recommend to their clients that reinforces what they are telling them. That's how this book can help you.

Buying this book at bulk discount pricing affords you several options. One: you can pass part of the discount on to your clients, saving them money and also and keep a little extra money for yourself. Two: increase your appointment or class charge by a few dollars and include the book in "what they get". Veterinarians can do the same for all new puppy or new dog appointments, especially dogs newly adopted from a shelter. This will be valued added for your clients. Three: sell the book at regular retail pricing in your facility. Four: make a donation of a quantity of books to an animal rescue group or shelter.

For more information about bulk pricing, email me at Info@AnimalBehaviorAssociates.com

2. Don't Get Left Behind!

Your Personal Invitation from Dr. Suzanne Hetts:

Join me in Behavior Education Network

The amount of information about pet behavior available now through the internet and other sources is staggering. It can feel – and actually is – at times overwhelming keeping up with scheduling clients, following up with them PLUS making time to keep current in your field and still have a life!

And an even bigger problem is being able to critically evaluate all the information and education available to you. I know from first-hand experience that results from recent research have not been accurately disseminated. Articles abound containing information that mislead readers about what the research studies actually found. And not only that, some research is methodologically flawed, but unless you have access to the original papers and know how to evaluate research methods and statistical analyses, you would have no way of knowing that the conclusions are suspect, or at least overstated.

That's just ONE of many benefits membership in Behavior Education Network provides you. Each month we critically review a research paper that is relevant to pet behavior and training. We've delved into papers ranging from the effects of pheromones, to different training methods, to effects of spaying and neutering. What we've found is often NOT what you've read from sources who haven't actually read the original research paper!

Each month we give you a Member Only webinar series – currently there are over 60 CEU approved webinar courses in BEN that you have immediate access to when you join. In addition, to Dr. Estep and me, past instructors have included Ms. Kathy Sdao, Dr. Alice Moon-Fanelli, Terry Ryan, Ms. Nancy Williams and more.

BEN members now also have access to the recordings of every monthly Chat with Certified Applied Animal Behaviorists (visit CAABChats.com for more information) as well. We also have a private Facebook group with all sorts of lively discussions. Members can share details about cases they wouldn't feel comfortable putting in an open group or forum. You can add your name to a searchable business directory and add BEN's member logo to your website.

With more open and personal access to Certified Applied Animal Behaviorists, links to and analysis of scientific articles, weekly Biscuits (tips and information you can put right to work during your next class or client) BEN membership gives you access to the science side of animal behavior you won't find in any other single place.

Because you bought this book, when you join BEN, I'll give you a month's free membership. When you join BEN, type the **coupon code "terrible"** in the shopping cart and you'll get 2 months of membership for the price of one. You can cancel your membership at any time, but to prevent the rare person from abusing this offer, your $25 for your two months of membership is non-refundable. You won't be billed for 30 days after you join.

Visit www.BehaviorEducationNetwork.com and join hundreds of other pet professionals who want to be on the cutting edge of knowledge about pet behavior and training.

Made in United States
Orlando, FL
01 October 2023

37473726R00115